Characteristics of effective early learning

Helping young children become learners for life

Characteristics of effective early learning

Helping young children become learners for life

Edited by Helen Moylett

Open University Press

Open University Press
McGraw-Hill Education
McGraw-Hill House
Shoppenhangers Road
Maidenhead
Berkshire
England
SL6 2QL

email: enquiries@openup.co.uk
world wide web: www.openup.co.uk

and Two Penn Plaza, New York, NY 10121-2289, USA

First published 2014

A catalogue record of this book is available from the British Library

ISBN-13: 978-0-335-26326-4
ISBN-10: 0-335-26326-7
eISBN: 978-0-335-26327-1

Library of Congress Cataloging-in-Publication Data
CIP data applied for

Typeset by Aptara, Inc.
Printed and bound by Ashford Colour Press Ltd, Gosport, Hampshire

Acknowledgements

As the editor I am very grateful to all the contributors for their enthusiasm in getting involved in sharing their expertise and to Fiona Richman and the publishing team for their support. We are all particularly indebted to the many children and practitioners whose ideas and experiences bring our writing to life and without whom this book would not have been written. On a more personal level I would also like to say a big thank you to Lesley Abbott who taught me so much – mainly about early years – but also about how to be an editor!

Praise for this book

"This is such a useful edition to other publications which clarify, enrich and expand on messages in the revised Early Years Foundation stage. A range of early years experts offer valuable insights on important topics linked to young children learning. The contributors write authoritatively drawing on historical studies as well as more current research. Authentic case studies vividly illustrate theoretical points.

Helen sets the stage beautifully, providing a rationale, structure and sequence to a book which truly and lovingly celebrates the processes of children's unfolding development."

Marion Dowling, Early Years Specialist and Vice President of Early Education

"An insightful and engaging read for students and professionals within the Early Years sector that brings alive the concepts of effective learning that underpin the Early Years Foundation Stage. The book provides an excellent synthesis of developmental and pedagogic research enabling readers to make connections between theory and practice. One of the great strengths of the book is the way in which young children are celebrated as active and powerful agents in their own learning. The book allows readers to reflect on how adults can build on this to ensure that the potential for learning within each child is fully supported through effective pedagogies as well as in more formal planning and assessment. The contributing authors bring a variety of perspectives and knowledge that combine to illuminate the principles behind effective early years practice and explore how these can be translated into meaningful and supportive experiences for children."

Dr Mary Wild, Principal Lecturer, School of Education,
Oxford Brookes University, UK

"What a wonderful sub-title 'Helping young children to become learners for life'. It is **so** refreshing to find, (among the plethora of new publications on child development) a book that really sees all children as 'rich children' and describes them as capable and confident learners. All the authors share their knowledge in a highly accessible manner which means I can recommend this book to both our practitioners and students undertaking first degrees and post qualifying courses.

The authors clearly identify the qualities and attributes of highly effective learners. They share the view that young children come into Early Childhood Education settings hungry to make sense of relationships and the world they are growing up in. They powerfully describe the kind of skilled educators that children deserve; educators who can harness children's energy, engage with their interests and extend their critical thinking."

Dr Margy Whalley, Director of the Pen Green Centre for Children
and Families and the Pen Green Research Base

Contents

Contributors

Di Chilvers is an advisory consultant, author and trainer in early childhood education having worked in the early years sector for over 35 years. Di works with settings, schools and local authorities across the country to support the development of good practice in the early years. Long term development projects include Talk for Reading, Observing Children's Thinking, Young Children Talking, Child Led Play and Learning and bespoke work with partners. Her latest book – *Creating and Thinking Critically: A Practical Guide to How Babies and Young Children Learn* (2013) – tells the 'story' of children's unique and inspirational thinking.

Clare Crowther is the Head of Norland Nursery in Bath. Clare's professional background in early years includes leading a large children's centre, the coordination of forest schools, and the training and continued professional development of the early years workforce to level 7. Clare has written several publications, and until recently wrote monthly articles for a leading nursery magazine.

Helen Moylett is an independent early years consultant and writer. She has been an early years teacher, a local authority senior advisory teacher and a senior lecturer in primary and early years education at Manchester Metropolitan University. In 2000 she left academia to become head of an early years centre. In 2004 she joined the National Strategies. She was centrally involved in developing the Early Years Foundation Stage as well as many of the National Strategies materials associated with it. Her most recent publication is *Active Learning* (2013). Helen is currently President of the British Association of Early Childhood Education (Early Education) and a Visiting Fellow of Oxford Brookes University.

Kim Porter is a part time school improvement partner as well as being an independent early years consultant. She had a key leadership role in the National Strategies working on the Every Child a Talker programme. Kim has wide experience of planning continuing professional development and support materials across all aspects of language and literacy from birth to 11, combined with raising outcomes for pupils through direct work with practitioners and a focus on improving teaching and learning, through modelling and peer coaching. Kim co-authored the Literacy Trust's Early Reading Toolkit audit and has written materials and resources to support young children's understanding of history.

Dr Sue Rogers is Head of the Department of Early Years and Primary Education at the Institute of Education, London. Her research interests include play, curriculum and pedagogy in early childhood, young children's perspectives and child-adult inter-action. She has published widely in the field of early childhood education includ-ing three books *Inside Role Play in Early Childhood Education: Researching Children's Perspectives* (2008, with Julie Evans), an edited collection on play pedagogy enti-tled *Rethinking Play and Pedagogy: Concepts, Contexts and Cultures* (2011) and *Adult Roles in the Early Years* (2012, with Janet Rose).

Judith Stevens is an independent writer, consultant and trainer. She has worked in the private and voluntary sectors as well being a teacher, maths coordinator and early years team leader. Following a long career in local authority advisory roles, Judith took on a leadership role in national programmes including Every Child a Talker. Most recent books include: *Foundations of Mathematics: An Active Approach to Number, Shape and Measures in the Early Years* (2013, with Carole Skinner) and *Maths Now: The Definitive Guide to Maths in the Early Years Foundation Stage* (2009). She has an interest in all aspects of mathematics, particularly maths outdoors and through stories, rhymes and role play.

Nancy Stewart is an independent writer, consultant and trainer. She has wide-ranging experience working with early years children and families across sectors and has lectured on early years foundation degree courses and served as assessor for Early Years Professional Status. While working for the National Strategies Nancy developed training and materials on early communication and language and play. Nancy has written and contributed to books on parenting and health. Her most recent books are *How Children Learn: The Characteristics of Effective Early Learning* (2011) and (with Helen Moylett) *Understanding the Revised EYFS* (2012). Nancy is on the national executive of TACTYC.

Dr David Whitebread is a senior lecturer in psychology and education at the Uni-versity of Cambridge. He is a developmental cognitive psychologist and early years specialist. Before entering higher education, he taught in early years and primary schools for 12 years. His current research projects include work on metacognition and self-regulation in young children's learning, and the impact of playful experi-ences on children's narrative skills. Other interests include evolutionary psychol-ogy, the application of cognitive neuroscience to early years education, and issues related to 'school readiness'. His publications include *Teaching and Learning in the Early Years* (3rd edition, 2008) and *Developmental Psychology and Early Childhood Education* (2011).

1 How young children learn: introduction and overview

Helen Moylett

The authors of this book believe that all children are born ready, able and eager to learn. We are passionate in our commitment to children's entitlement to become good learners whatever their personal or family circumstances and believe that the best early years pedagogy rests on deep understanding of child development. This book explores some aspects of how habits of mind are formed as our brains and bodies develop and we come to understand ourselves as learners. The role of adults in this process is key. When young children are left to their own devices in a stimulating learning environment most will learn through playing and exploring – but this is not enough. It is through the active intervention, guidance and support of a skilled adult that children make the most progress in their learning. This does not mean pushing children too far or too fast, but instead meeting children where they are emotionally and intellectually. It means being a partner with children, enjoying with them the power of their curiosity and the 'skill, will and thrill' of finding out what they can do.

The 'skill, will and thrill' represent the characteristics of effective early learning.

- playing and exploring – the *skill* to get engaged
- active learning – the *will* to keep going
- creating and thinking critically – the *thrill* of discovery

Readers in England will recognize these characteristics as specifically Early Years Foundation Stage (EYFS) terminology. The revised EYFS Statutory Framework (DfE 2012: 1.10) states:

> In planning and guiding children's activities, practitioners must reflect on the different ways that children learn and reflect these in their practice. Three characteristics of effective teaching and learning are:
>
> - **playing and exploring** – children investigate and experience things, and 'have a go';

- **active learning** – children concentrate and keep on trying if they encounter difficulties, and enjoy achievements; and
- **creating and thinking critically** – children have and develop their own ideas, make links between ideas, and develop strategies for doing things.

It would be easy to miss the importance of this brief statement, which makes it mandatory for practitioners to respond not just to *what* children learn but also to *how* they learn. There is also a requirement for each child's end of key stage summative assessment (the EYFS Profile) to include a short commentary on how they demonstrate the characteristics of effective early learning.

Of course these ideas about how children learn are not new and nor are they confined to children learning in England. The EYFS itself has been influenced by research and practice from across the world including Reggio Emilia, New Zealand and the United States. The revised EYFS Statutory Framework has the limitations of any government document and, although it serves to some extent as an organizational tool, the writers of this book draw on many traditions and their own wide experience as well as *Development Matters in the Early Years Foundation Stage* (Early Education 2012), the non-statutory guidance which expands and explains the characteristics and the areas of learning (the how and what children learn) in practice. In some cases this is necessary to make sense of the framework which suffers from having been written by policy makers who commendably wanted to keep it brief but sometimes did not understand the significance of what they left out in order to achieve this aim. For example, 'playing with what they know' unfortunately does not appear in the statutory framework in any form of words, even though pretend play (as Sue Rogers explains in Chapter 3) marks a move to a higher level of thinking and connects to logical and abstract thought – all very important in becoming a good learner.

Under 'A Unique Child' *Development Matters* sets out what one might expect to see children doing when playing and exploring, being active in their learning and creating and thinking critically (see Figure 1.1). (In the document there are further columns with suggestions for 'Positive Relationships: what practitioners could do' and 'Enabling Environments: what practitioners could provide'). It can be seen that the three characteristics interact with each other and overlap in practice. In play and exploring, for instance, a child will be actively involved and motivated as well as creating and thinking critically.

In the UK today's practitioners are the inheritors of a long tradition of good early years practice based on play and hands-on experiences for young children where practitioners aim to increase children's independence, choice and control over their own learning. But many practitioners have been struck by how much they themselves still use the same learning strategies as adults – in other words we could easily drop the 'early' from the title and they could be the characteristics of effective lifelong learning. We refine and develop our characteristics in various ways as we get older, but essentially we use the same strategies as babies.

Playing and exploring – engagement

Finding out and exploring
    • Showing curiosity about objects, events and people
    • Using senses to explore the world around them
    • Engaging in open-ended activity
    • Showing particular interests

Playing with what they know
    • Pretending objects are things from their experience
    • Representing their experiences in play
    • Taking on a role in their play
    • Acting out experiences with other people

Being willing to 'have a go'
    • Initiating activities
    • Seeking challenge
    • Showing a 'can do' attitude
    • Taking a risk, engaging in new experiences, and learning from trial and error

Active learning – motivation

Being involved and concentrating
    • Maintaining focus on their activity for a period of time
    • Showing high levels of energy, fascination
    • Not easily distracted
    • Paying attention to details

Keeping on trying
    • Persisting with activity when challenges occur
    • Showing a belief that more effort or a different approach will pay off
    • Bouncing back after difficulties

Enjoying achieving what they set out to do
    • Showing satisfaction in meeting their own goals
    • Being proud of how they accomplished something – not just the end result
    • Enjoying meeting challenges for their own sake rather than external rewards or praise

Creating and thinking critically – thinking

Having their own ideas
    • Thinking of ideas
    • Finding ways to solve problems
    • Finding new ways to do things

Making links
    • Making links and noticing patterns in their experience
    • Making predictions
    • Testing their ideas
    • Developing ideas of grouping, sequences, cause and effect

Choosing ways to do things
    • Planning, making decisions about how to approach a task, solve a problem and reach a goal
    • Checking how well their activities are going
    • Changing strategy as needed
    • Reviewing how well the approach worked

Figure 1.1   A Unique Child: observing how a child is learning.

Recent research in brain development and psychology provides evidence of the remarkable learning abilities of babies. They may be vulnerable and need care and protection, but they have strong drives to be competent, to engage with others and make meaning. They show curiosity, make choices and are persistent. In other words they are able to use most of the same strategies that will support them as learners all their lives, such as imitating others, noticing patterns and making predictions. These characteristics can be helped or hindered by the experiences and interactions children have.

> When they are encouraged and supported to follow their curiosity, to feel the satisfaction of meeting their own challenges, to think for themselves, and to plan and monitor how they will go about their activities, they become self-regulated learners who later outstrip children who may have developed more early subject-based knowledge but are more passive in their learning.
>
> (Moylett and Stewart 2012: 10)

An acknowledgement of the importance of what we now know about self-regulation lies at the heart of the renewed emphasis on the characteristics in the EYFS. As well as managing feelings and behaviour, self-regulation involves attitudes and dispositions for learning and an ability to be aware of one's own thinking. Children are born playful and curious and need time and space to develop and learn through their natural desires to engage with other people and the environment in which they live. This process is represented in *Development Matters* (Early Education 2012) as a simple sum (see Figure 1.2).

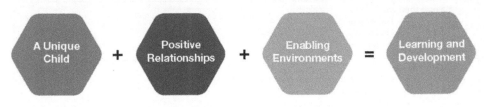

Figure 1.2 The process of Learning and Development.
Source: Early Education (2012).

A Unique Child, Positive Relationships, Enabling Environments and Learning and Development are the four themes of the EYFS and are inter-related:

> **A Unique Child** actively drives their own learning, reaching out and making sense of their experiences with people and world around them. Within warm and loving **Positive Relationships** the child experiences

emotional safety which is the bedrock to learning about how to be a person, and joins the world of learning with and from others. **Enabling Environments** provide the stimulating outdoor and indoor experiences – in settings and at home – which challenge children, respond to their interests and meet their needs. The result of these three elements interacting together is the child's **Learning and Development.**

(Moylett and Stewart 2012: 6, original emphasis)

The practice guidance in the EYFS includes more information and ideas about how to value early childhood as a stage in its own right and tune in to where children are, supporting and challenging them without rushing them through crucial stages of their emotional, cognitive and physical development.

Respect for children as active, playful learners may seem at odds with the idea of early learning goals and setting out *what* children will learn by the time they are 5. Many young children in reception classes cannot meet all the early learning goals but are still good learners. It is to be hoped that the new requirement to notice and report on *how* children learn may reinforce practitioner confidence in prioritizing learning to learn.

After all, several years into the twenty-first century, research and practice have confirmed the claims that John Holt was making in the 1960s in books such as *How Children Fail*, that since we cannot predict what children will need to know in a changing world, it is senseless to try to fill them with our current knowledge. Instead, we should be focusing on *how* they learn and help them to love learning so much that they will be able to cope with change and learn whatever they need.

Being in love with learning starts with people being in love with us. Every few seconds another human is born into the world. How long each baby survives and whether they lead happy lives between birth and death will depend on many factors, the most important being whether they are loved and cared for in their early years. The fact that well-being underpins learning has been known about for many years, but developments in neuroscience have confirmed that early attachment relationships are crucial for brain development (Gerhardt 2004). Warm, positive interactions and exploring the world with the senses build a brain that can trust and care for others, manage emotions and learn effectively. Repeated positive experiences build the strong connections that will remain for life. When babies work out that they can depend on and trust a caregiver (usually, but not always, their mother) who is consistently responsive and sensitive to their physical and emotional needs, they have what is called a 'secure attachment'. Babies can also form close bonds with a small group of other people who know them well. These relationships are vital to their learning and development and explain why the key person role in settings is so important.

As babies we need and seek constant repetition of acts of being loved, trusted and given control to begin to understand ourselves and others. The most fundamental task of a baby is to learn how to meet her needs. When her signals are recognized and she receives what is often referred to as a 'contingent' response based on what she actually needs, rather than on what the carer thinks she might or should need, she will calm, feel secure and begin to be able to regulate her own behaviour.

These early childhood experiences physically determine how the brain is 'wired'. At birth, babies have all, or most, of the brain cells they will ever have but connections between these cells are incomplete; early experiences wire the connections. Repetition of experiences strengthens them. The first three years see the most rapid changes and this is when the brain is most flexible and prepared to learn. The number of connections can go up or down by 25 per cent or more, depending on the environment. Connections that aren't used are pruned.

Secure attachment supports us to be effective learners as well as happier, healthier people and this has been recognized in various government commissioned reports which argue for more investment in the early years (Field 2010; Marmot 2010; Allen 2011). The subtitle of this book, 'helping young children become effective learners for life', underlines the importance of that investment. Although clearly the early years sector needs more financial investment, in the context of this book we are talking about what adults invest in terms of time, knowledge and skills when they work with children. If we want a return on that investment that means more children become lifelong learners, then we have to think seriously about whether we are really focused on long term gains or short term quick fixes.

The dangers of concentrating on short term fixes at the expense of deep learning have been amply demonstrated by one of the strongest sources of evidence we have about the long-lasting effects of how we are encouraged to learn when we are young – the HighScope Perry Pre-School evaluations. The heart of the HighScope approach is supporting children to plan, carry out and review their own learning, motivated by their own ideas and interests and supported by skilled practitioners as appropriate. The original HighScope project has been the subject of a rigorous longitudinal study following children who took part in the programme until they were over 40 years old. One strand of the research compared children who had been in the project with those who attended 'direct instruction' (behaviourist/formal, practitioner led) pre-schools.

Children who had attended direct instruction settings showed early achievement gains in English and maths but as the children got older that advantage disappeared and the balance shifted. By the age of 15, children from the direct instruction group were half as likely to read books, twice as likely to have committed 'delinquent acts' and were far more likely to be socially and emotionally troubled than children from HighScope and traditional nursery schools. By the age of 23 the direct instruction group were almost four times more likely to have been arrested and had almost eight times the rate of emotional impairments. They were about half as likely to have graduated from college.

When, at age 40, the HighScope group were compared with children who did not go to any pre-school provision it was found that they exhibited less anti-social and criminal behaviour and were less likely to be drug users. They were far more likely to be doing voluntary work in the community, have stable marriages and higher earnings. It is significant that these HighScope children were all born in poverty and had been identified as at risk of academic failure. In other words social disadvantage does not have to be a life sentence – good quality early years settings can make a difference.

Both HighScope in the US and the Effective Provision of Pre-School Education (EPPE) in the UK focused on children in provision for 3- to 4-year-olds. Other studies have linked babies' persistence at various ages with parenting style and toddler outcomes. For example one study compared babies' persistence at 6 and 14 months with their mothers' 'teaching style'. They found that mothers who provide access to stimulating objects, are sensitive and responsive to children's emotions and support children's behaviours just above their current level may foster both persistent behaviour and advanced cognitive development in the future. They suggest that practitioners should work with at risk children and families to develop strategies that support the development of persistence (active learning: keeping on trying) as early as possible (Banerjee and Tamis-LeMonda 2007).

These findings are supported by some research (McClelland et al. 2012) which interestingly compares the long term effects of early persistence with the long term effects of reading and maths ability. The study followed 430 children from preschool age to adulthood. Contrary to researchers' expectations they found that maths and reading ability did not have a significant effect on whether students gained a university degree. But those who could concentrate and persist at the age of 4 were almost 50 per cent more likely to have completed a degree course by the age of 25.

The big message from all this research and indeed from every chapter of this book, is that what practitioners do in the early years matters for life. As individuals we cannot stop children being born into poverty and disadvantage, but our practice can improve their long term outcomes and support the aspirations of recent UK government policy to intervene early and prevent poor children becoming poor adults (Field 2010; Allen 2011). The formal behaviourist view that all learning is shaped by the teacher (as in the direct instruction pre-schools of the HighScope evaluation) does not have long term impact on aspects of life which help us sustain our learning, loving and earning power. Concentrating in the early years on how children learn by supporting their well-being and learning strategies enables them to be more self-reliant, active learners who can exercise control over their own lives. If we concentrate on what, rather than how children learn, any short term gain soon wears off and these children are then left with insufficient emotional and cognitive self-regulation resources to manage their lives successfully. It was the concentration on how we learn that ensured the HighScope children were more likely to go to college, rather than filling them up with knowledge that is soon forgotten.

A theme of this book that can be seen in every chapter is the importance of relationships and well-being underpinning learning. As *Every Day's a Learning Day* so eloquently puts it: 'Health and Wellbeing . . . is about learning how to lead healthy and active lives, becoming confident, happy and forming friendships and

Social and emotional development Well-being	**Playing and exploring** *engagement*	**Ready**	Skill
	Active learning *motivation*	**Willing**	Will
	Creating and thinking critically *thinking*	**Able**	Thrill

Figure 1.3 Emotional and cognitive self-regulation.

relationships with others that are based on respect . . . *It is also about managing feelings and having the skills to meet challenges, make good choices and manage change'* (Education Scotland 2012: 4, emphasis added).

Figure 1.3 represents the way in which to see the whole picture of self-regulating learners, the social and emotional side must be included. We cannot think if we do not feel safe, cared for and well. If there is not emotional safety, we cannot take risks and push our boundaries. And we learn within relationships – with both adults and peers.

In New Zealand (Carr 2001) children's dispositions for learning are the main focus of assessment, and are described as stages of 'ready, willing, able'. This fits well with the characteristics of effective learning.

Playing and exploring (engagement) Children seek out and engage in first-hand and imaginative experiences, gathering the material to feed their learning and being prepared to take a risk in new experiences – they are *ready* to learn.

Active learning (motivation) Children invest concentration and energy in following their interests, seek the satisfaction of meeting their goals and show perseverance in the face of difficulty – they are *willing* to learn.

Creating and thinking critically (thinking) Children have their own ideas of how to do things, they make sense of their experiences by linking ideas, and they choose how to do things including thinking about their goals and strategies and monitoring their success – they are *able* to learn.

Alternatively they have the *skill* in playing and exploring, the *will* and the *thrill* of doing and thinking – recognizing their own power as learners.

This is a book which recognizes both the powerful learning capacities of young children and the need for practitioners to see themselves as learners too, who work hard on forming positive relationships and providing enabling environments for children – in order to be like the inspiring women that Tina Bruce (1999: 36) praises and thanks for her own lifelong interest in learning: 'These were not quick fix, get there early, get good outcomes, good SATS results, League Table teachers. These were help-you-to-be-long-term-forever-learner kinds of teacher.'

Although there are lots of examples from practice here, this is not a 'top tips' book, nor a textbook where every chapter follows the same format; nor does it pretend to cover every aspect of early years. It concentrates on sharing what we believe is important about how children learn while recognizing that everyone's practice is rooted in their values, beliefs and knowledge and supported by theory and experience and the social and cultural context in which they work. Therefore every writer has a different 'voice' and every reader will 'hear' those voices differently. As editor my wish is that readers find both support and challenge to be advocates for early childhood learning as important in its own right and as the foundations of the future.

The chapters are placed in what seems a logical order – starting with this general overview and then moving from self-regulation generally, through each of the characteristics in particular, then on to observing, assessing and planning for how children learn followed by how adults set up and maintain a learning community, and finishing with moving the learning into Key Stage 1. There are overlaps between chapters, and themes which are common, however each chapter stands alone and readers can dip in and out in any order without losing the main plot of the importance of children learning how to learn and adults supporting and extending that learning.

In Chapter 2 David Whitebread presents an overview of research on self-regulation and how practitioners can most effectively support the development of children's metacognitive skills and positive emotional/motivational dispositions towards themselves as learners. He draws on his involvement with the Cambridgeshire Independent Learning project to examine the possibilities for a pedagogy for self-regulation in early childhood education where children initiate activities making the decisions about what to play, where and with whom; setting their own goals and challenges and self-directing the learning and resolving problems. Making thinking and learning visible through communication and language is a theme. In order for this to work four principles have to be recognized. The first is the need for emotional warmth and security. Closely related to this is emotional and intellectual control alongside cognitive challenge and opportunities for children to articulate their learning.

Chapter 3 by Sue Rogers considers the ways in which play and exploratory behaviours change and develop in children from birth to 6 and suggests ways in which adults might engage with and support children's understanding of the world around them during this critical period, both indoors and outdoors. The importance of relationships is highlighted throughout with reference to attachment and attunement in the earliest forms of play, sensorimotor activities, the growth of imagination and theory of mind, and the development of highly complex social play. The EYFS Statutory Framework states: 'Each area of learning and development must be implemented through planned, purposeful play'. There has been much debate in the early years sector about what 'planned, purposeful play' might look like and what the balance of adult-led and child-initiated activity should be. Sue points out that, although play provision needs to be planned carefully to ensure that children have access to a wide range of possibilities and opportunities, if the purpose is more important than the act of play then it probably isn't play! Sue argues that young children need to take risks and explore a wide range of materials, environments and social situations in order to approach learning with confidence. Sue is explicit about the benefits of this approach as children make the transition into Key Stage 1 – a theme which is picked up again by Kim Porter in Chapter 8.

In Chapter 4 Nancy Stewart explores active learning, which is all about motivation in learning. She underlines the importance of children's commitment, energy and perseverance towards achieving a goal. She refers to social psychology theories about the impact of developing orientations towards either performance or mastery goals, and of intrinsic versus extrinsic motivation. The strand of 'being involved and concentrating' is related to Ferre Laevers' involvement signals and the concept of flow, as children follow their own fascinations to satisfy their curiosity and their own purposes. Perseverance, described in the EYFS as 'keeping on trying', is linked to self-efficacy and autonomy. The third strand of 'enjoying achieving what they set out to do' refers to the importance of intrinsic motivation, linked to a mastery orientation and the satisfaction of the drive for competence. Nancy explores Carol Dweck's work on mindset and the need to encourage a growth mindset by praising and recognizing children's efforts and power to evaluate their own learning (mastery), rather than focusing on their achievements (goals). Implications for early years practice are identified in relation to each strand of active learning.

In Chapter 5 Di Chilvers picks up the thread of the drive for competence and the ways in which playing and exploring create the ideal context for creating and thinking critically. She focuses on how we recognize and understand creative and critical thinking in babies, toddlers and young children and how this supports their development as thinkers and learners. The careful and sensitive observation of children is a key theme. Case studies illustrate the language of thinking and the many elements that are combined together in holistic patterns of learning; for example, children developing their own ideas and possibilities, setting and solving problems, making connections between ideas, playing with ideas and using conversational language to interpret their thinking, ask questions and try things out. The development of the imagination is stressed and links made to Anna Craft's work on 'small c' creativity and possibility thinking. Play and active learning are discussed as contexts for creating and thinking critically. Di stresses the importance of the observation, assessment and planning cycle in supporting practice.

This is the theme that is developed in more depth by Judith Stevens in Chapter 6. The chapter focuses on the inclusion of the characteristics of effective learning in assessment and the shift from only *what* children learn to *how* they learn – a new component in the EYFS Profile. Overall, the need for flexibility in planning and tuning into young children's current enthusiasms and fascinations is seen as key. Judith points to the danger of getting so focused on 'learning intentions', that practitioners may miss the key, significant learning that is going on all around them. She gives an example of being so busy 'observing' how children are ordering numbers from zero to ten, as they peg number cards they have made onto a washing line as part of an adult planned experience, that other more significant behaviours are missed. Judith provides many rich examples of children learning and how practitioners can tune into both children and their learning. She emphasizes the need to work closely with parents, valuing their contributions to the observation, assessment and planning cycle.

Clare Crowther also has a community focus in Chapter 7. The previous chapters all reflect on the crucial role of the adults who work with children in supporting and extending children's abilities as learners. While sharing some of this approach, Clare explores in more detail the ways in which adults have to be learners themselves in order to establish a setting as a true community of learners where children, staff and parents learn together in a supportive environment and understand how the characteristics of effective learning apply both to the children and themselves.

Using examples from her own setting Clare unpacks the joys and challenges involved in successfully leading and changing the learning ethos in order to make it easier for children and adults to be active, playful creative learners and thinkers. Leadership and management at any level are about learning and development. Settings, and the adults working in them, grow and develop in response to positive relationships and enabling environments – just like the children. Clare unpacks some of her leadership and management decisions as she and the staff develop and improve their relationships and environment for learning. The chapter questions thinking on mixed age groups and explores what a positive emotional environment really looks like and means for all who are part of it. Clare and her colleagues have worked hard to create something akin to what Bruce describes as

> a feeling of calm, an anchored feeling, a settled feeling in a group which felt like a real community, and yet they seemed to do this in order to jolt you and make you rethink or think anew in quantum leaps. It was exciting to learn with them. You had a sense you would never be the same again, and you weren't!
>
> (Bruce 1999: 36)

Tina Bruce's teachers were not fettered by routine and they were inspiring because they were learners themselves who saw the children and themselves as part of a community. They were in love with learning and understood that the way to get children to be good learners was to share that love. In order to do that of course you have to see yourself as a thinker. As Lilian Katz dryly observes: 'If teachers want their young pupils to have robust dispositions to investigate, hypothesize, experiment, conjecture and so forth, they might consider making their own such intellectual dispositions more visible to the children'(Katz 1995: 65). Making our own adult thinking and the joy of that thinking visible to the children is a recurring theme in this book and is picked up again by Kim Porter in the final chapter.

Practitioners often worry about what will happen when children who are used to being independent, competent learners, excited by their own learning, move on to the next phase of their education. Globally the emphasis in education has moved away from giving information and towards supporting learning skills – what Guy Claxton has called 'building learning power'. Learning to learn has been identified as crucial for personal success and participation as citizens in an inclusive society and projects all over the world are focusing on the learner as a whole person. Yet, despite all this ongoing interest and activity, we have too many children whose capacities to be citizens of the twenty-first century are being wasted, like Emily's, a 15-year-old GCSE student: 'I guess I could call myself smart. I mean I can usually get good grades. Sometimes I worry though that I'm not equipped to achieve what I want, that I'm just a tape recorder repeating back what I've heard. I worry that once I'm out of school and people don't keep handing me information with questions . . . I'll be lost (Claxton 2004: 1). As Claxton puts it, 'Emily sees herself as ready for a life of tests, but not the tests of life' (p. 1). Emily appears to have no sense of agency as a learner and to be sadly aware of her learned helplessness – to have what Carol Dweck (2006) calls a 'fixed mindset'.

In the final chapter Kim Porter considers the potential of the characteristics of effective learning to ensure children make the most of their primary school experience and don't just prepare for tests like Emily. Kim addresses the issue of effective transition from EYFS into Key Stage 1, asking: is there still a place for play and exploration in Key Stage 1? What would active learning in primary school look like? How can practitioners provide opportunities for creating and thinking critically in Year 1 and beyond? In answering these questions Kim considers how primary schools can create a climate in which active learning is promoted and children are authentically engaged and suggests that good progress and good outcomes are most likely when teachers and school communities understand that lifelong learning aptitudes and attitudes are at the heart of planning, provision and practice. She cites the new Ofsted inspection framework as a helpful approach in England presenting increased possibilities for creative and innovative practice in Key Stage 1 classrooms.

Kim reminds us that, despite the popular work of people like Guy Claxton and Ken Robinson, there is still much learned helplessness and teacher direction in primary and secondary schools. Hearteningly she concludes her chapter with two case studies illustrating the characteristics of effective learning in action in Year 1. The second case study ends with Jack and Billy, telling the story of their learning: 'They breathe out after this joint stream of words and look so pleased with themselves they are practically glowing. The teachers are stunned.'

The teachers are stunned because Jack and Billy are two children to whom they have not been paying sufficient attention. This is easy to do in a busy classroom – as Judith Stevens reminds us in Chapter 6, one can be so focused on observing one's own learning intentions that one misses the children's.

When discussing really paying attention Nancy Kline links the quality of our attention-giving skills to the creation of space to think. 'The quality of your attention determines the quality of other people's thinking . . . Attention, the act of listening with palpable respect and fascination, is the key to a Thinking Environment' Kline (1999: 36 and 37). Practitioners who really pay attention to children and their involvements will not force children to be interested in anything but will gently encourage many different interests and let children lead their own learning. Luckily for Jack and Billy they went to Forest School and 'Jack now knows of different ways to get around challenges, he is less frustrated with classroom life, and sometimes speaks up knowing that the teacher has a different view of him as inventive, able and capable and he is beginning to believe that anything is possible.'

We have to let children guide us if we are to help them become lifelong learners and we have to be learners with them – all of them, not just those who arrive in our settings and schools showing us how ready, willing and able they are. This investment of our time, care and attention will pay dividends for the children and also the adults for, as Vivian Gussin Paley (2004: 8) says, 'It is in the development of their themes and characters and plots that children explain their thinking and enable us to wonder who we might become as their teachers.'

References

Allen, G. (2011) *Early Intervention: The Next Steps*, An Independent Report to Her Majesty's Government. London: Cabinet Office.

Banerjee, P.N. and Tamis-LeMonda, C.S. (2007) Infants' persistence and mothers' teaching as predictors of toddlers' cognitive development, *Infant Behavior & Development*, 30: 479–91.

Bruce, T. (1999) In praise of inspired and inspiring teachers, in L. Abbott and H. Moylett (eds) *Early Education Transformed*. London: Falmer.

Carr, M. (2001) *Assessment in Early Childhood Settings Learning Stories*. London: Paul Chapman.

Claxton, G. (2004) *Learning to Learn: A Key Goal in a 21st Century Curriculum*, A discussion paper for the Qualifications and Curriculum Authority. London: QCA.

DfE (Department for Education) (2012) *Statutory Framework for the Early Years Foundation Stage: Setting the Standards for Learning, Development and Care for Children from Birth to Five*. http://www.foundationyears.org.uk/early-years-foundation-stage-2012/ or http://www.education.gov.uk/aboutdfe/statutory/g00213120/eyfs-statutory-framework (accessed 1 January 2013).

Dweck, C. (2006) *Mindset: The New Psychology of Success*. New York: Ballantine Books.

Early Education (2012) *Development Matters in the Early Years Foundation Stage*. London: Early Education. www.early-education .org.uk and for download at http://www.foundationyears.org.uk/early-years-foundation-stage-2012/ (accessed 20 December 2012).

Education Scotland (2012) *Everyday's a Learning Day: Birth to 3 Years*. Glasgow: Education Scotland.

Field, F. (2010) *The Foundation Years: Preventing Poor Children Becoming Poor Adults,* The report of the Independent Review on Poverty and Life Chances. London: Cabinet Office.

Gerhardt, S. (2004) *Why Love Matters: How Affection Shapes a Baby's Brain*. London: Routledge.

Gussin Paley, V. (2004) *A Child's Work*. Chicago: University of Chicago Press.

Holt, J. (1964) *How Children Fail*. London: Penguin.

Katz, L. (1995) *Talks with Teachers of Young Children*. New Jersey: Ablex Publishing Company.

Kline, N. (1999) *Time to Think: Listening to Ignite the Human Mind*. London: Ward Lock.

Marmot, M. (2010) *Fair Society, Healthy Lives: Equity from the Start*. London: UCL, Institute of Health Equity.

McClelland, M., Acock, C., Piccinin, A., Rhea, S.A. and Stallings, M. (2012) Relations between preschool attention span-persistence and age 25 educational outcomes, *Early Childhood Research Quarterly*, 28: 314–24.

Moylett, H. and Stewart, N. (2012) *Understanding the Revised Early Years Foundation Stage*. London: Early Education.

2 The importance of self-regulation for learning from birth
David Whitebread

Introduction

Within developmental psychology, it is now well established that by far the most significant determinant of children's success as learners is their development of what are termed 'metacognitive skills' (i.e. their awareness, knowledge and control of their own mental processes) and positive emotional and motivational dispositions towards themselves as learners. These elements combined have come to be referred to as the development of 'self-regulation'. While these abilities were once thought to be late developing, emerging in children only towards the end of their primary schooling, a wealth of recent research has shown that they emerge and can be seen to develop from a much younger age. Indeed, as we shall see, early indications of abilities which underpin self-regulation have now been detected in children when they are only a few months old. As I want to argue in this chapter, there is therefore now good evidence to suggest that it is self-regulatory abilities which lie at the core of children's development as effective, powerful learners, from birth.

What also makes this research particularly exciting for those of us involved in early childhood education is the further evidence that self-regulation skills are very heavily influenced by young children's early experience. In other words, early years educators are in a unique position to have a major beneficial influence on children's development, their realization of their full potential as learners and a whole range of positive life outcomes.

In this chapter I therefore want to review some of this important research, including some of my own, illustrating the precise components of self-regulation, the early emergence of these skills and dispositions in very young children and the implications for a pedagogy for self-regulation in early childhood education. The chapter is therefore organized into four sections, dealing with the following topics:

- the nature and characteristics of self-regulation;
- the early emergence of self-regulation in young children, including cognitive, emotional, social and motivational elements;

- the importance of developing self-regulation for children's success as learners and for their emotional well-being;
- environmental and social interaction factors which support children in developing self-regulation and implications for practice in early childhood education settings.

The nature and characteristics of self-regulation

Three theoretical and research traditions have contributed to the development of our understandings concerning the nature of self-regulation abilities and dispositions. These arise from the cognitive psychology tradition, originally inspired by the Swiss developmentalist Jean Piaget, which has developed the notion of 'meta-cognition', the sociocultural tradition, within which the theoretical ideas of the Russian Lev Vygotsky have been pre-eminent, and the social cognitive theories of motivation, inspired by the ideas and research of the influential American Albert Bandura.

Perhaps the simplest way to convey what is meant by 'self-regulation', and the contribution of each of these traditions to this phenomenon, is to ask you to undertake a short task. Carry out the following subtraction sums in your head (i.e. without writing anything down), but then write down what you did in your head to work out the answer:

A) 58 – 23
B) 72 – 37
C) 104 – 97

The first thing to note is that, as an adult, you were able to select a way (or 'strategy') for doing these subtractions. In other words, you have *knowledge*, in your long-term memory, of how to do this type of sum, and this is something you could not do when you were a very young child, but have learnt or developed over the years.

Second, you probably have more than one strategy for doing subtractions, and you may have used more than one of these in undertaking these three sums. For example, many people would do sum A by taking 3 from 8 (the units) and then 2 from 5 (the tens). However, in sum B, because 7 is greater than 2, many people change their strategy, so they might, for example, count on from 37 to 40, then from 40 to 70, and then from 70 to 72, and add up the three amounts to get the answer. In sum C, again, as the numbers are close together, and as they fall either side of 100, many people will just count on in ones from 97 to 104, or visualize the two numbers on a number line with 100 in the middle, and see that they need to add 3 (because 97 is 3 below 100) to 4 (because 104 is 4 above 100).

There are, of course, many others strategies you could have used which would work perfectly well, and which you have devised and developed over the years. In other words, as an adult, you have a repertoire of strategies, and you are able to select which one to use, for any particular task, based on your knowledge of such tasks, what works for you, and so on; i.e. you exercise *control* over your own mental processing.

And finally, not only can you do these subtractions in your head, but, simultaneously, you are able to *monitor* what you are doing and can report it afterwards. In other words, you are aware of your own mental processes. In addition to allowing you to articulate what you have done, this monitoring process is vitally important, as it allows you to keep track of where you are in the task, to detect errors, to be aware of how easy or difficult you are finding the task, and so on. In turn, the information derived from monitoring can then be used to exercise various control functions including correcting errors, going back to an earlier stage of the task, changing or modifying strategies and increasing concentration.

The dominant model used to represent the interactions of metacognitive knowledge, control and monitoring is that developed by Nelson and Narens (1990). Here these internal mental processes are represented as a feedback loop between two spheres of activity, which occur simultaneously within the brain, which they refer to as the META level (in which metacognitive knowledge of relevant strategies is stored and referred to) and the OBJECT level (in which the actual task, in this case the subtraction sum, is undertaken). The Monitoring function consists of information about where you are up to in the task, how well it is going, and so on, flowing from the OBJECT level to the META level; and the Control function consists of instructions from the META level to the OBJECT level either to continue with the procedures as planned, or to change strategy in some way if a difficulty or an error has been detected (see Figure 2.1).

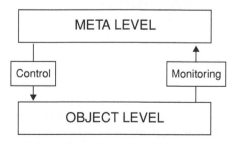

Figure 2.1   Nelson and Narens' model of metacognition.

According to the theoretical models of the self-regulated learner developed within the three research traditions mentioned above, you have learnt how to become an able learner, thinker and social being in the world because you have developed the 'metacognitive' knowledge, monitoring and control you used when doing the subtraction sums, and apply these whenever you undertake any kind of mental task, solve any type of problem, exercise your creativity, manage and negotiate a social situation, or manage and control your own emotions and motivations. The 'metacognitive' research has been concerned with exploring the internal mental processes involved in these achievements; the sociocultural, Vygotskian research has explored the social and educational processes which support the learning and development of these abilities; and the motivational research has explored the processes which provide the mental energy or effort to undertake this learning.

Within the cognitivist tradition, the term 'metacognition' was originally coined by Flavell (1979) to describe a phenomenon he observed in a series of investigations concerning the development of children's memory abilities, and the strategies they used to help them remember (Flavell et al. 1966). In these experiments, he presented children in the age range 5–10 years with a set of objects, and then pointed to some of the objects in a set order. After a delay of 20 seconds or so, during which he observed the behaviour of the children, he then asked the children to indicate the objects he had pointed to, and in the correct order. Not surprisingly, the older children were more likely to be observed using an appropriate strategy (in this case, 'verbal rehearsal', involving saying or whispering the names of the objects to themselves) and were much more successful than the younger children at the memory task.

The gradual emergence of a wide range of such cognitive strategies, related to many different areas of learning, had been documented in children by this time, and it was generally considered that strategies were adopted by children when they became able to use them. However, Flavell realized that it might not be that simple. It could be that the younger, 5-year-old children were capable of using the verbal rehearsal strategy, but were just not aware of it. So, he taught it to them and showed that they were capable of verbally rehearsing and, when they did so, they performed as well on the memory task as the 10-year-old children. However, when given a similar task a few days later, many of the 5-year-olds failed to use verbal rehearsal and again failed the task. Flavell termed this a 'production' deficit, i.e. the children could use verbal rehearsal but failed to produce it spontaneously in relation to an appropriate task.

Early years practitioners will recognize this phenomenon. Young children can often do something one day but, when it is presented to them subsequently in a slightly different form, the connection is not made with the earlier experience and they are not able to apply what they have learnt to the new situation. In these landmark studies, Flavell demonstrated that this behaviour is not a consequence of children's inabilities to use particular strategies before a certain age. The children in his studies did not lack the basic cognitive resources to verbally rehearse. Rather, he argued, their difficulties should be conceptualized as a 'metacognitve' problem. In relation to Nelson and Narens' model, represented in Figure 2.1, the limits on what the children could do were located in the monitoring and control processes, and at the META level, rather than at the simply cognitive OBJECT level.

This early work, and subsequent research establishing the fundamental significance of metacognitive abilities for learning, has led to an explosion of research concerned with the development of metacognition in children, teenagers, students and adults of all ages. This has included, in recent years, some initial studies in the development of metacognitive abilities in young and very young children, to which we will return in the next section.

Paralleling this work concerned with the internal mental processes of metacognition, has been a body of research inspired by the theoretical work of Vygotsky (1978, 1986) concerned with the social processes through which children learn, and learn to self-regulate. The fundamental idea here is that, at any point in time, and in relation to any area of understanding or skill, the developing child has two levels of capability. The first, developmentally lower level consists of what the child is currently able to do on their own. The second, higher level, is what they are able to do with some help or guidance from an adult or more experienced peer. The ideas, understanding and skills or abilities which need to be mastered to move from the lower to higher level are referred to by Vygotsky as the 'zone of proximal development' (see Figure 2.2).

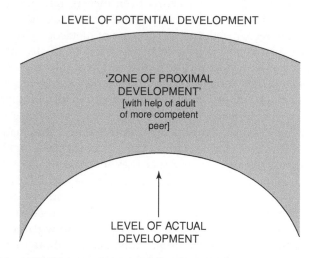

Figure 2.2 Vygotsky's 'zone of proximal development'.

Think, for example, of a young child attempting a jigsaw which is slightly too difficult for them. On their own they will fail and give up. However, an adult working with them can model useful ways of proceeding (e.g. collecting and joining up the edge pieces, looking at the picture and then looking for pieces that match items seen in it), can make suggestions and give prompts (can you find the corner pieces? Shall we find all the blue bits for the sky?), can ask strategic, 'metacognitive' questions which direct the child to think through the task (would it help to sort the pieces in some way? Which part of the jigsaw should we start with? Does some of it look easier and some harder?) and so on.

This type of supportive interaction, referred to in the research literature as 'scaffolding', has been shown to be consistently beneficial to children's learning. One key element here, however, has been shown to be the sensitivity with which the adult hands over the regulatory role to the child, as the child gradually acquires the skills and understandings they need to be able to do the task on their own. The contingency with which the adult withdraws, just doing enough at all times to enable the child to proceed with the task, and consequently supporting the child's autonomous action in relation to the task, has been consistently shown to be crucial in this regard (Wood et al. 1976). Where this is done skilfully, the child is supported in making the transition from being 'other-regulated' to being 'self-regulated' in relation to that area of learning. This area of research, which demonstrates and explores one of the key elements in the processes by which children can be supported to develop their self-regulation abilities, has led to significant findings in relation to supportive styles of interaction, and the role of language in the development of self-regulation. These are issues to which we will return in the final section of this chapter.

The final element which has recently been increasingly integrated in models of self-regulation relates to theory and research concerned with motivation. It has been increasingly recognized that the exercise of metacognitive skills and self-regulation requires mental effort. Work in this area was originally inspired by Bandura's (1997) theory and research related to the notion of self-efficacy, which refers to the human need to feel competent, the positive feelings which we experience when we achieve something new, and the consequences for our approach to new tasks when we have an underlying belief in our own competence to tackle new challenges. A further significant contribution in this area is that made by Dweck's work concerned with what is termed 'attribution' theory (Dweck and Master 2008). This concerns to what we attribute our successes and failures. Put simply, she has demonstrated that some individuals attribute their successes and failures on tasks to factors outside their control, such as fixed ability, luck and so on. Failure on a task, resulting in this type of attribution, leads to a range of negative consequences, including avoiding such tasks in future, quickly giving up when any difficulty is encountered, and so on. In contrast, other individuals attribute their level of performance to the amount of effort they put into a task or activity. For these people, failure on a task leads to renewed effort, increased concentration and perseverance. A considerable body of research has now shown the very strong links between self-efficacy, attributional beliefs and other related aspects of motivation to children's developing self-regulation.

Theory and research which was initially quite separate from these cognitively focused motivational theories, but is now increasingly recognized as a crucial element in motivational aspects of self-regulation, concerns children's developing abilities to regulate their emotions. Research in this area, for example, has built on early work showing that securely attached children are more playful, more positively curious about new objects and experiences, more able to cope with change and happy to take risks and make mistakes. Extensive research on the relationships between attachment and emotional self-regulation has been reviewed by Calkins and Leerkes (2011). In other related work with preschool children, Eisenberg et al. (2011) have reviewed work related to the relations between effortful control (an early element of self-regulation, as we will review in the following section) and the development of emotion regulation and well-being. In a review of five qualitative studies with older students, Pekrun et al. (2002) found that positive emotions were consistently related to effort, interest, use of elaboration strategies and self-regulation and negatively related to irrelevant thinking. Negative emotions showed the opposite pattern, being negatively related to interest, effort, elaboration strategies and self-regulation and positively related to irrelevant thinking and external regulation.

The gradual integration of theories and research related to emotional development, motivation and cognitive aspects of self-regulation has recently been accomplished through the development of a new and widely accepted, overarching model of human motivation, originally developed by Deci and Ryan (2008) which is termed 'self-determination theory'. This proposes three basic human needs for feelings of autonomy, competence and relatedness. The first two needs clearly relate to feelings of control and self-efficacy, and relatedness (a feeling of being valued and loved by significant others) clearly relates to the work on attachment and emotion. Within this model, the majority of the latest research has focused on the notion of autonomy, or the child's sense of 'agency', 'empowerment' or control. Reeve et al. (2008) have provided a recent review of the extensive work showing the strong links between feelings of autonomy and self-regulation development. This clearly relates to the early work of Wood et al. (1976) and much more recent work (see the final section of this chapter), concerned with autonomy promoting practices in interactions between adults and children. There are highly significant insights emerging from this work which provide strong guidance for early childhood educators keen to promote children's self-regulation. In summary, the established view of self-regulation which is currently widely adopted within the research community is that expressed by two of the leading members of this research community. The modern, integrated view of self-regulation is that it consists of 'The process whereby students activate and sustain cognitions, behaviours, and *affects*, which are systematically oriented toward attainment of their goals' (Schunk and Zimmerman 1994: 309, original emphasis).

This leads me onto one final point concerning what is meant by self-regulation and, particularly, what is not meant. In some of the literature, and certainly in some commentaries written upon it for the educational profession, there is an unfortunate confusion between self-regulation and compliance. Within Schunk and Zimmerman's definition, however, it is important to notice that we are talking about children's ability to organize themselves mentally in relation to the achievement of *their* goals. Of course, many young children will share or happily adopt their teacher's goals as their own. However, some will not, for various reasons which are beyond the remit of this chapter. Being self-regulated, however, is not the same as being compliant or conventionally a well-behaved, 'good' pupil. This is a vitally important point as children who are non-compliant, but have well-developed self-regulation abilities, and children who are compliant, but who are disposed to be dependent on adults, and have not developed good self-regulation abilities, are both done a disservice through this confusion.

The early emergence of self-regulation in young children

Extensive recent research has established that if children are observed undertaking tasks which are age appropriate and meaningful to them, the early building blocks of metacognitive and self-regulatory abilities can be discerned in very young children. At the turn of the new millennium, Bronson (2000) provided a comprehensive review of research up to that date on self-regulation in children from birth to the end of the primary school phase, covering cognitive, emotional, motivational and social areas of development and, in a recent paper, a colleague and I have reviewed progress in this research since that date (Whitebread and Basilio 2012). Table 2.1 provides a summary of the key findings available at that time of Bronson's review in relation to early cognitive self-regulation.

Table 2.1 Early development of cognitive self-regulation

From 0 to 12 months old	Focuses attention on specific others, objects and own activities (reaching, grasping, manipulating objects)
	Notices regularities and novelties in the social and physical environment
	Begins to participate and predict sequences
	Begins to initiate behaviour sequences with people and objects
	Notices effects of own actions
From 12 to 36 months old	Wants predictable routines and resists change
	Can choose among a limited number of alternatives
	Goal directed behaviour
	Begins to notice and correct errors in goal directed activities
	Uses an increasing number of strategies to reach goals
	Shows cognitive organization by matching, sorting and classifying
From 3 to 6 years old	Can engage in a wider range of cognitive activities
	More able to carry out multi-step activities
	More able to control attention and resist distraction
	Can learn to use more advanced problem solving strategies
	More able to choose tasks appropriate for own level of skill

Source: Adapted from Bronson (2000).

In the subsequent decade or so, this work has been considerably developed and now focuses predominantly of three areas of early cognitive control, or 'executive functioning', which have been established as fundamental ways in which the human brain operates and learns. In an influential more recent review, Garon et al. (2008) identified these as working memory (the ability to hold information in mind while operating on it); inhibitory or effortful control (the ability to stop an initial, prepotent, automatic or perceptually driven response and replace it with a response related to an internal goal or thought); and cognitive or attentional flexibility and focus (the ability to control attention, to focus on key elements of a task, and to switch attention when required). Early evidence of each of these abilities has been reported during the first year of life, when they are strongly dependent, of course, on environmental factors such as novelty. From the second year onwards, however, progress has been documented in each of these abilities as children become able to handle more information for longer periods of time, and their attention and behaviour are increasingly under control and independent of context.

Hofmann et al. (2012) have produced one of a number of recent papers demonstrating ways in which these early executive functions form the building blocks for the beginnings of cognitive self-regulation. A range of studies have now demonstrated, for example, very early examples of children's emerging abilities, at 10 months, to use something learnt in one context and apply it to another (analogical learning); to request help appropriately, at 14 months, based on recognition of the limits of their own abilities; and to recognize and correct errors (at 18 months) in manipulative play.

In a paper reporting a study carried out in the early 1970s, concerned with 3–6-year-old children's memory abilities in meaningful tasks, a Russian psychologist, Z.M. Istomina (1975), included a number of transcripts of the children's performance which illustrate beautifully the early emergence of cognitive self-regulation. The task required the child to remember a list of five food items which were needed for a pretend lunch party (set out in one corner of a large room) so that she could ask the shopkeeper (at a pretend shop in the far corner of the room) for the correct items. Here is Istomina's record of the performance of a 5-year-old girl called Alochka on this task:

> Alochka (five years, two months) was busily engaged in preparing lunch, and several times reminded the experimenter that she needed salt.
>
> When it was her turn to go to the store, she asked, with a busy expression on her face:
>
> "Z. M., what should I buy? Salt?"
>
> The experimenter explained to her that this was not all and named four more items that were needed. Alochka listened attentively, nodding her head. She took the basket, the permission slip and money and went off, but soon came back.

"Z. M., I have to buy salt, milk, and what else ?" she asked. "I forgot."

The experimenter repeated the items. This time Alochka repeated each word after the experimenter in a whisper and, after saying confidently, "Now I know what I had forgotten," went off.

In the store, she went up to the manager and, with a serious expression, correctly named four items, with slight pauses between each.

"There is something else, but I forgot" she said.

(Istomina 1975: 25–6)

We can clearly see here evidence of emerging metacognitive awareness and cognitive self-regulation in Alochka. Throughout she is aware of what she has remembered and what she has forgotten. To begin with she tries the simple strategy of 'nodding her head' for each item on the list, but quickly realizes this hasn't worked. So, the second time, she uses a different strategy, 'repeat(ing) each word after the experimenter in a whisper', and this is much more successful. Aloshka is clearly an able 5-year-old, but already, at this very young age, she is showing some important elements in the process of developing into a very successful self-regulated learner.

Similar advances have taken place in our understandings about the achievements of young children in the emotional, social and motivational (affective) domains, and these are similarly reported in detail in my previous paper (Whitebread and Basilio 2012). Once again, this later review builds on the work of Bronson (2000). Table 2.2 provides a summary of the key findings available at the time of Bronson's review in relation to early affective self-regulation.

In the last decade research in this area has focused on the development of two key phenomena. First, we now have good evidence that young children develop what is commonly referred to as a 'theory of mind', or an understanding that other individuals have a mind like their own, and their own perspectives, at a much younger age than was previously thought. This understanding is of vital importance to the developing child's emotional well-being, forming the basis for effective social interaction and sensitivity, empathy, the development of friendships and positive relationships with adults. Following Piaget's early work suggesting young children are 'egocentric' (i.e. not able to take on the perspectives of others), and early research using language-based laboratory tasks, children were not thought to develop these understandings until around 5 years of age. However, recent work focusing on where younger children look rather than what they say, and using non-verbal tasks, has demonstrated that children as young as 15 months appeal to mental states, such as beliefs, to explain the behaviour of others. In imitation tasks, children of a similar age have also been shown to imitate precisely the actions of a machine or robot, but to do what a human model appeared to intend to do (e.g. place a toy on the edge of a table), rather than what they actually did (e.g. apparently accidentally drop the toy on the floor) (Meltzoff 2011).

Table 2.2 Early development of social-emotional regulation

From 0 to 12 months old	Regulation of arousal and sleep/wake cycles Responsive interaction with others Attempts to influence others Begins to anticipate and participate in simple routines Responsiveness to emotional expressions of others
From 12 to 36 months old	Increasing voluntary control and voluntary self-regulation Growing ability to comply with external requests and awareness of situational demands Increasing assertiveness and desire for independent action Increasing awareness of others and the feeling of others (empathy) Some spontaneous helping, sharing and comforting behaviours Increasing awareness of social rules and sanctions Increasing ability to inhibit prohibited activities and delay upon request
From 3 to 6 years old	More capable of controlling emotions, abiding by rules, and refraining from forbidden behaviours More capable of using language to regulate own behaviour and influence others More interest in peers and peer acceptance, so more apt to regulate self in relation to peers Can learn more effective interaction strategies Can engage in dramatic play with roles and rules Begins to talk about mental states of self and others Better understanding how others may feel Can engage deliberate helping, sharing, and comforting behaviours Internalizing standards of behaviour Developing more stable prosocial (or antisocial) attitudes and behaviours

Source: Adapted from Bronson (2000) and Kopp (1982).

The second main focus of research in the area of affective self-regulation has concerned children's developing inhibitory and effortful control abilities. This work has used 'Do's and Don'ts' and 'Go/NoGo' tasks (where the child has to perform an action, or not, depending on a rule) and delay of gratification tasks, such as the famous marshmallow task, where the child has to resist touching or eating an attractive toy or sweet. As in all areas of self-regulation development, considerable progress has been found in children within the first few years of life in their performance on these tasks. Significant individual differences have also been found, however, but a number of studies have shown that early secure attachments are strongly associated with these affective self-regulation abilities. We will return to the issue of environmental and social factors which seem to support the early development of children's self-regulation in the final section.

Once children enter educational institutions, of course, the demands on their cognitive and affective self-regulatory abilities are considerable. There is strong evidence, as we shall see in the next section, that well-developed self-regulatory abilities help children to make a smooth transition into pre-school and early schooling.

At the same time, however, the more challenging opportunities that a high quality early childhood educational setting can offer can also significantly enhance all young children's early self-regulatory abilities. This will be the topic of the final section of this chapter.

In my own research, within the Cambridgeshire Independent Learning (C.Ind.Le) project (Whitebread et al. 2005, 2007, 2009), I have particularly explored the development of 3–5-year-olds' self-regulatory abilities. In this study we worked with 32 nursery and reception class teachers, and the children in their classes (just under 1500 children altogether) and we video-recorded around 700 self-regulatory 'events' in these settings. One outcome of this study was the production of an observational instrument, the Checklist of Independent Learning Development (CHILD 3–5), which includes 22 statements, in the areas of cognitive, emotional, prosocial and motivational self-regulation (see details in Whitebread 2009). These statements were selected from a longer list, derived from their research literature, of children's self-regulatory achievements in this age range, and indicate the abilities which distinguish high from low, or well from poorly, self-regulated children at this stage of their development. This instrument has subsequently been translated into a number of languages, and has been extensively used in research and by practising early childhood educators, both within the UK and internationally. As well as providing a valuable and teacher-friendly assessment tool related to individual children's development, it has also been effectively used as a basis for discussions about children's development with parents, and as an audit of practice supporting self-regulation development within classes and settings.

The importance of developing self-regulation

I have devoted a good part of this chapter to describing the nature of metacognition and self-regulation, and their development in young children, because it is vitally important that early childhood educators have a deep understanding in this area. This arises from two now widely accepted findings from a considerable body of research. First, that metacognitive and self-regulatory abilities are the single most powerful determinants of children's academic success and a range of positive life outcomes; and, second, that these abilities are significantly affected by environmental and social interaction factors in children's early experience. Early childhood educators are, as a consequence, in a position to make a very positive difference to children's developmental outcomes. This section addresses the findings regarding the significance of developments in this area, and what we can do about it is addressed in the final section.

There are essentially three types of evidence that have convinced the research community, and early childhood policy decision makers, internationally, about the importance of this area. First, there have been a number of longitudinal studies looking at the short-term and long-term outcomes of different types of pre-school and early childhood education provision. (see Chapter 1). The HighScope research and evaluation established that seven dollars of Federal funding was saved for each dollar spent on the project. As a consequence, not surprisingly it had a dramatic impact on governments internationally and education policy makers. It also led to renewed research to attempt to identify which features of such a high quality early education programme contributed to these outcomes. In the UK the more recent Effective Provision of Pre-School Education (EPPE) project (Sylva et al. 2004), for example, was set up to address this question and has provided important complementary evidence.

What emerges as significant about effective early educational environments are features which crucially support young children's developing self-regulation. These environments offer real intellectual challenge with emotional support, and put the child very much in control of their own learning. In the HighScope regime, for example, the central model of learning is the 'plan, do and review' cycle. Each child plans their activities for the session or the day in a small group with an adult educator, often referred to as a 'key worker'. The children then move off to carry out their planned activities, and later return to review progress again with their small group, again supported by their key worker.

This pattern of working also builds in purposeful adult-child and child-child conversations, which oblige and offer children the opportunity to reflect upon and talk about their learning. Sylva et al. (2004) particularly identified, within the highest quality settings, the occurrence of episodes of 'sustained shared thinking' between adults and children, where adults supported children's ideas and helped the children to extend and develop them. As we shall see, providing opportunities for children to talk authentically about their learning is an important component in helping them to develop as self-regulating learners. This is also not just a matter of cognitive activity, but has important emotional and motivational elements. What all the high quality early years regimes identified by Sylva and Wiltshire (1993) did was to help children develop what they term a 'mastery' orientation to learning and to themselves (see Chapter 4). Children in high quality early years environments developed secure feelings of self-efficacy. Such children grew to believe that, through effort, they could solve problems, understand new ideas, develop skills and so on. They felt in control of their environments and confident in their abilities.

The second, very considerable body of evidence consists of studies that have looked at the role of metacognitive and self-regulation abilities in a wide range of cognitive and affective areas of development. In cognitive areas such as maths, reading, writing, thinking skills and problem-solving, and in affective areas such as social relationships, tolerance, cooperation, impulsiveness, addiction and eating disorders, self-regulation skills are of vital significance. Some studies have looked specifically at the immediate short term outcomes of children's individual differences in this area. Essentially, these studies are often focused on the consequences for young children's transition into their early years of pre-school and schooling. So, for example, in the area of cognitive self-regulation, Blair and Razza (2007) found that, out of a range of possible factors, including a measure of their general intelligence, the level of inhibitory control shown by 3–5-year-olds from low-income families most clearly predicted their reading and maths abilities a year later. In relation to affective areas, Denham and Burton (2003) showed that emotion regulation in preschool children predicted their peer status, friendship, academic competence, self-image and emotional well-being.

Finally, there have been a number of meta-analyses conducted of studies devoted to establishing the effectiveness of all kinds of educational interventions. Hattie (2009) is pre-eminent in this area, having reported the results of 800 such meta-analyses related to a huge range of educational interventions conducted all over the world. His conclusion from this vast analysis is that a range of approaches which teach children metacognitive strategies, or which support children's metacognitive awareness by encouraging them to talk about their learning, such as reciprocal teaching or peer tutoring, are among the most effective in relation to academic outcomes. Within the UK, Higgins et al. (2011) carried out a similar exercise, but just looking at around 50 meta-analyses within the UK, particularly focusing on interventions directed towards children from disadvantaged backgounds who would qualify for the Pupil Premium. The conclusions were very similar to Hattie's (2009). The most successful interventions focused on supporting children to monitor their own learning or to work collaboratively with peers in ways which required them to articulate what they understood or had learnt.

Supporting children's self-regulation in early childhood education

I have written elsewhere setting out some of the basic characteristics of early childhood education settings which appear to most effectively support young children's developing self-regulation (see Whitebread and Coltman, 2011; Whitebread, 2012). The main four elements I have stressed involve establishing an emotionally warm, secure and encouraging classroom climate, providing tasks which are appropriately challenging, giving children a real sense of control or autonomy in relation to their activities and their learning, and making the processes of learning 'visible' by encouraging children to talk about their learning. I hope at least some of the underlying rationale for each of these points has emerged from the foregoing review of aspects of the research in this area.

In this final section I want to review some of the key pieces of research which support these general conclusions, and hopefully to deepen and extend them a little by reference to some of the very interesting specific findings which have emerged. Two bodies of research have made particular contributions in this regard: research looking at classroom practices which support self-regulation, and studies of interactions with much younger children with their parents (usually their mothers). Research in classrooms has examined the characteristics of effective interventions and the consequences of naturally occurring differences between teaching practices. This research has mostly been undertaken with slightly older primary classes, but there are key features of effective practice which emerge that can equally well be applied to working within early childhood settings. These relate to the emotional and motivational context of the classroom and the significance of social processes in self-regulation development.

As regards the first point, Perry (1998), for example, observed 2nd and 3rd grade classrooms' literacy activities over a period of six months. Based on her observations she concluded that classrooms supporting self-regulation were characterized by challenging and open-ended writing activities, opportunities for children to control the level of challenge and opportunities for them to engage in self-assessment, autonomy support (through being taught strategies to undertake certain types of task), encouragement of positive feelings towards challenge, an emphasis on personal progress and seeing mistakes as opportunities for learning.

Most of the work on social processes in classrooms has focused on the production of 'metacognitive talk' by teachers and on pedagogical practices which support children's talk about their learning. Typically, effective self-regulation interventions have involved the teacher making metacognitive and learning strategies explicit and encouraging children to reflect upon and talk about their learning. The value of the first of these arises from the established finding, first identified experimentally by Flavell in the early studies we reviewed in the first section of this chapter, that young children often fail to produce an appropriate strategy in relation to a task, even though they have previously shown themselves to be capable of performing it. Subsequent research demonstrated one reason why this might occur. Fabricius and Hagen (1984), for example, explored the use of an organizational strategy with 6- and 7-year-olds. Following improved performance some of the children attributed this to the use of the strategy, but others thought they had recalled more because they had looked longer, used their brains more, or slowed down. While only 32 per cent of the children in the latter group transferred the use of the strategy to a second recall task, 99 per cent of those who explicitly recognized the impact of the organizational strategy they had been taught did so. In other words, it is clear that, in the early stages of self-regulation development, we need to do some of the metacognitive work for the children. For example, when introducing a new way of doing something, which helps the children perform at a higher level, we need to explicitly discuss why this worked. And when introducing a new task, we need to explicitly remind the children of when they faced something similar before, and what worked then.

Ornstein et al. (2010) have supported this view in a study in which they monitored the amount of 'metacognitive talk' among 1st grade teachers in mathematics lessons. Such talk included teachers making suggestions of memory strategies the children could use, asking metacognitive questions aimed at eliciting strategy knowledge from the children, such as 'how could you help yourself to remember this?', and so on. A natural variation in this kind of 'memory relevant' talk was recorded among the teachers, ranging from 0–12 per cent of their talk during the lessons. Also recorded was the co-occurrence of memory talk and memory demands, i.e. the percentage of times that the metacognitive talk occurred when the children were required to remember something. A highly statistically significant difference was reported between children in classes with high and low occurrences of this kind of metacognitive talk, particularly where it was related to memory demands. Most impressively, they found that children's improved strategy use and ability to remember relevant mathematical facts related to these differences at the end of the 1st grade, and were still present at statistically significant levels three years later, at the end of the 4th grade.

A wide range of self-regulation interventions have essentially developed types of activity which are likely to encourage children to talk about and reflect upon their learning. These include cooperative groupwork (where children work in pairs or small groups to undertake a task, or produce something together), peer-tutoring (where one child is asked to teach something they know or can do to another child), 'self-explanations' (where children are asked to explain their reasoning, or that of another – for example, in Philosophy for Children or general discussions), self-assessment (where children select work they are proud of to put in their portfolio, or say what they are pleased about in something they have done), and debriefing (where an activity is reviewed, perhaps supported by photographs).

In the C.Ind.Le study, reported earlier, a key finding was the frequent occurrence of children in the 3–5 age range demonstrating metacognitive and self-regulatory abilities during playful activities, particularly in constructional and pretence play (Whitebread et al. 2007). The self-regulatory activities and talk during construction play tends to relate to cognitive problem solving. In this context we often observe what is referred to as 'private speech', where children commentate to themselves on their activities. This seems to be a kind of bridge between the speech they experience in situations of adult scaffolding and their use of inner speech, or thought, in order to guide and regulate their activity. Berk et al. (2006), among others, have provided rich examples of children demonstrating and practising self-regulatory abilities during pretence play. In a recent study of complex social pretend play, a colleague and I reviewed the now extensive evidence of the numerous self-regulatory opportunities within this kind of play, as children guide the play narrative forward either in character ('Oh dear, the baby's crying!') or by stepping momentarily out of character ('OK, you pretend you're the baby and you're crying because you're upset') (Whitebread and O'Sullivan, 2012). This is perhaps the most sophisticated type of play in which young children engage, and one that many children struggle to perform well. As such, it is a prime example of where a skilful adult can participate, taking on some of the regulatory role, and, if they are able to sensitively withdraw as the children become more competent, it can be an excellent vehicle to support a range of linguistic and self-regulation abilities.

I want to finish by reviewing evidence concerning children's language development and self-regulation. In a way, we might characterize these as the two twin pillars on which children's development as learners is founded. A number of studies have shown that they are intimately related in early childhood. An American study of 120 toddlers in New England, for example, showed strong relationships between vocabulary size at 14, 24 and 36 months and a range of observed self-regulatory behaviours (e.g. the ability to maintain attention on tasks; the ability to adapt to changes in tasks and procedures) (Vallotton and Ayoub 2011).

Many of the studies contributing to this area of research have investigated early interactions between children and their mothers, often in the context of what have been termed 'joint attention episodes', where mother and child are jointly focused on a particular object or event, and communicate pre-verbally, or non-verbally, or talk about it together. In a recent article, Brinck and Liljenfors (2013) have reported evidence that metacognitive and self-regulatory abilities can be identified between 2 and 4 months of age in episodes of dyadic interaction between mothers and their infants. In such episodes, they argue, the adult is both a model for the child and a source of feedback guiding their early attempts at cognitive control. We know from a range of research that the amount of time children spend in episodes of joint attention is directly related to their language development and, thus, to their self-regulation development also. Schaffer (2004: 299) gives a very clear example of such an episode and its key features:

> Take the following common scenario of a mother and her 2-year-old child playing with a set of toys: the child inspects the toys, selects one of them picks it up and begins to play with it; the mother thereupon starts talking about that toy; she may name it, point out its uses and features, comment on the child's previous encounters with it or similar toys, and in this way verbally enlarges on the specific topic that the child is attending to at that moment.

In addition to differences in the time young children spend in such episodes with their parents, there are also, however, significant differences in the sensitivity, or responsiveness, of parents or caregivers to their children, and this also impacts upon language development. Some adults are much more aware of the child's pointing gestures or gaze as indicators of their focus of attention. Furthermore, while many adults behave as described by Schaffer, following and responding to the focus of the attention of the child, others tend to attempt to switch the child's attention to their own focus of interest. Not surprisingly, the former 'attention-following' strategy, building on the child's current interest and attention, has been found to support language development much more effectively than the 'attention-shifting' approach, with consequent outcomes also for the child's self-regulation development.

Other research has also investigated the style and content of mother's speech during joint activities with their young children. Bibok et al. (2009), for example, have reviewed a range of evidence concerning the relative frequencies of 'directive' and 'elaborative' utterances in mother's talk in joint attention episodes. Directive utterances are those which directly request a specific action or behaviour, while elaborative utterances provide contextual information of the type listed above by Schaffer, or give reasons for actions, or in other ways encourage the child to think beyond the immediate context of the task at hand. The more frequent use by mothers of elaborative styles of speech has been found to be related to young children's executive function development which, as we discussed earlier, is a key building block in the early emergence of self-regulation.

Conclusion

It is still early days in our investigations of the fascinating and complex processes of metacognition and self-regulation, their very early emergence in young children, right from birth, and their exciting and rapid development throughout early childhood. As I hope I have shown in this chapter, however, while we have much to discover, the research so far in this area has revealed illuminating and important insights into the early cognitive and affective aspects of self-regulation development and some of the environmental factors which impact upon it. Its importance in determining developmental outcomes for young children, both in the short and long terms, cannot be overestimated. At the same time, it is clear that the quality of the environments and experiences we provide for young children within early childhood educational contexts can have a profound effect on these developments. In particular, we need to pay attention to the emotional climate of our settings, so that the young children in our care feel secure and valued, to the extent to which we support children's feelings of autonomy and competence, and to the quality of the talk we provide when we interact with them in playful and conversational episodes.

Children are born into the world full of curiosity, eager to make sense of their experiences, to interact with and learn from their parents and other carers, to set themselves challenges and to achieve their goals. We can be of enormous help to them in this endeavour and it is my contention that the research reviewed in this chapter is beginning to make a significant contribution to helping us to understand how we should go about this. The ultimate goal of any teacher, of course, should be that their students grow into capable, independent learners who no longer need their help and guidance. If you leave the room, and come back a few minutes later, and all of the children are still fully engaged in their activities and have not realized you have been away, then you are probably getting it mostly right. Good luck with the endeavour.

References

Bandura, A. (1997) *Self-efficacy: The Exercise of Control*. New York: W.H. Freeman.
Berk, L.E., Mann, T.D. and Ogan, A.T. (2006) Make-believe play: wellspring for development of self-regulation, in D.G. Singer, R.M. Golinkoff and K. Hirsh-Pasek

(eds) *Play = Learning: How Play Motivates and Enhances Children's Cognitive and Social-Emotional Growth*. Oxford: Oxford University Press.

Bibok, M.B., Carpendale, J.I.M. and Muller, U. (2009) Parental scaffolding and the development of executive function, in C. Lewis and J.I.M. Carpendale (eds) Social Interaction and the Development of Executive Function, *New Directions for Child and Adolescent Development*, 123: 17–34.

Blair, C. and Razza, R.P. (2007) Relating effortful control, executive function, and false belief understanding to emerging math and literacy abilities in kindergarten, *Child Development*, 78: 647–63.

Brinck, I. and Liljenfors, R. (2013) The developmental origin of metacognition, *Infant and Child Development*, 22: 85–101.

Bronson, M. (2000) *Self-regulation in Early Childhood*. New York: Guilford Press.

Calkins, S.D. and Leerkes, E.M. (2011) Early attachment processes and the development of emotional self-regulation, in K.D. Vohs and R.F. Baumeister (eds) *Handbook of Self-regulation: Research, Theory and Applications*, 2nd edn. New York: Guilford Press.

Deci, E.L. and Ryan, R.M. (2008) Self-determination theory: a macrotheory of human motivation, development and health, *Canadian Psychology*, 49(3): 182–5.

Denham, S.A. and Burton, R. (2003) *Social and Emotional Prevention and Intervention Programming for Pre-schoolers*. New York: Plenum.

Dweck, C.S. and Master, A. (2008) Self-theories motivate self-regulated learning, in D.H. Schunk and B.J. Zimmerman (eds) *Motivation and Self-regulated Learning*. Mahwah, NJ: Lawrence Erlbaum.

Eisenberg, N., Smith, C.L. and Spinrad, T.L. (2011) Effortful control: relations with emotion regulation, adjustment and socialization in childhood, in R.F. Baumeister and K.D. Vohs (eds) *Handbook of Self-regulation: Research, Theory and Applications*, 2nd edn. New York: Guilford Press.

Fabricius, W.V. and Hagen, J.W. (1984) Use of causal attributions about recall performance to assess metamemory and predict strategic memory behaviour in young children, *Developmental Psychology*, 20: 975–87.

Flavell, J.H. (1979) Metacognition and cognitive monitoring: a new area of cognitive developmental inquiry, *American Psychologist*, 34: 906–11.

Flavell, J.H., Beach, D.R. and Chinsky, J.M. (1966) Spontaneous verbal rehearsal in as memory task as a function of age, *Child Development*, 37: 283–99.

Garon, N., Bryson, S.E. and Smith, I.M. (2008) Executive function in preschoolers: a review using an integrative framework, *Psychological Bulletin*, 134(1): 31–60.

Hattie, J. (2009) *Visible Learning: A Synthesis of 800 Meta-analyses Relating to Achievement*. London: Routledge.

Higgins, S., Kokotsaki, D. and Coe, R (2011) *Pupil Premium Toolkit: Summary for Schools*. London: Sutton Trust. http://www.suttontrust.com/education-endowment-foundation/toolkit/ (accessed 26 April 2013).

Hofmann, W., Schmeichel, B.J. and Baddeley, A.D. (2012) Executive functions and self-regulation, *Trends in Cognitive Sciences*, 16(3): 174–80.

Istomina, Z.M. (1975) The development of voluntary memory in preschool-age children, *Soviet Psychology*, 13: 5–64.

Meltzoff, A.N. (2011) Social cognition and the origins of imitation, empathy, and theory of mind, in U. Goswami (ed.) *The Wiley-Blackwell Handbook of Childhood Cognitive Development*, 2nd edn. Malden, MA: Wiley-Blackwell.

Nelson, T.O and Narens, L. (1990) Metamemory: a theoretical framework and new findings, in G. Bower (ed.) *The Psychology of Learning and Motivation: Advances in Research and Theory*, Vol. 26. New York: Academic Press.

Ornstein, P.A., Grammer, J.K. and Coffman, J.L. (2010) Teachers' 'Mnemonic Style' and the development of skilled memory, in H.S. Waters and W. Schneider (eds) *Metacognition, Strategy Use and Instruction*. New York: Guilford Press.

Pekrun, R., Goetz, T., Titz, W. and Perry, R. (2002) Academic emotions in students' self-regulated learning and achievement: a program of qualitative and quantitative research, *Educational Psychologist*, 37: 91–105.

Perry, N. (1998) Young children's self-regulated learning and contexts that support it, *Journal of Educational Psychology*, 90(4): 715–29.

Reeve, J., Ryan, R., Deci, E.L. and Jang, H. (2008) Understanding and promoting autonomous self-regulation: a self-determination theory perspective, in D.H. Schunk and B.J. Zimmerman (eds) *Motivation and Self-regulated Learning*. Mahwah, NJ: Lawrence Erlbaum.

Schaffer, H.R. (2004) *Introducing Child Psychology*. Oxford: Blackwell.

Schunk, D.H. and Zimmerman, B.J. (eds) (1994) *Self-regulation of Learning and Performance: Issues and Educational Applications*. Hillsdale, NJ: Lawrence Erlbaum.

Sylva, K. and Wiltshire, J. (1993) The impact of early learning on children's later development: a review prepared for the RSA inquiry 'Start Right', *European Early Childhood Education Research Journal*, 1: 17–40.

Sylva, K., Melhuish, E.C., Sammons, P., Siraj-Blatchford, I. and Taggart, B. (2004) *The Effective Provision of Pre-School Education (EPPE) Project: Technical Paper 12 – The Final Report: Effective Pre-School Education*. London: DfES/Institute of Education, University of London.

Vallotton, C. and Ayoub, C. (2011) Use your words: the role of language in the development of toddlers' self-regulation, *Early Childhood Research Quarterly*, 26: 169–81.

Vygotsky, L.S. (1978) *Mind in Society: The Development of Higher Psychological Processes*. Cambridge, MA: Harvard University Press.

Vygotsky, L.S. (1986) *Thought and Language*. Cambridge, MA: MIT Press.

Whitebread, D. (2012) *Developmental Psychology and Early Childhood Education*. London: Sage.

Whitebread, D. and Basilio, M. (2012) The emergence and early development of self-regulation in young children, *Profesorado: Journal of Curriculum and Teacher Education, Monograph issue: Learn to learn. Teaching and evaluation of self-regulated learning*, 16(1): 15–34.

Whitebread, D. and Coltman, P. (2011) Developing young children as self-regulated learners, in J. Moyles, J. Georgeson and J. Payler (eds) *Beginning Teaching, Beginning Learning: In Early Years and Primary Education*. Maidenhead: Open University Press.

Whitebread, D. and O'Sullivan, L. (2012) Preschool children's social pretend play: supporting the development of metacommunication, metacognition and self-regulation, *International Journal of Play*, 1(2): 197–213.

Whitebread, D., Anderson, H., Coltman, P. et al. (2005) Developing independent learning in the early years, *Education 3–13*, 33: 40–50.

Whitebread, D., Bingham, S., Grau, V., Pino Pasternak, D. and Sangster, C. (2007) Development of metacognition and self-regulated learning in young children: the role of collaborative and peer-assisted learning, *Journal of Cognitive Education and Psychology*, 6: 433–55.

Whitebread, D., Coltman, P., Pino Pasternak, D. et al. (2009) The development of two observational tools for assessing metacognition and self-regulated learning in young children, *Metacognition and Learning*, 4(1): 63–85.

Wood, D., Bruner, J. and Ross, G. (1976) The role of tutoring in problem-solving, *Journal of Child Psychology and Psychiatry*, 17: 89–100.

3 Playing and exploring
Sue Rogers

Introduction: setting the scene

> It takes creativity and commitment to get down on the floor and attentively and actively engage a toddler in pretense; such investment fosters developmental advances in children. It appears that children's play is children's work, but [adults] play can repay children some welcome fringe benefits.
>
> (Bornstein et al. 1996)

In a study of mother and toddler play and its impact on cognitive development, Bornstein and his colleagues suggest that adults have much to offer children's play, with the important caveat that to be most effective, adults should adopt a playful stance with the children, entering into the game rather than over- or re-directing the play or, alternatively, over-emphasizing its realistic and instrumental features. Similarly, Parker-Rees (2007) argues for practitioners in early years settings to engage in playful interactions with babies and toddlers in the way that many parents do naturally. From a review of research on imitation in infants, he concludes that 'reciprocal imitation with familiar partners reminds us that our delight in the company of other people lies at the very heart of the uniquely human process of intentional pedagogy' (Parker-Rees 2007: 11). Perhaps we should not be surprised that this 'delight in the company of other people' and the positive affect this can engender, strengthens bonds and familial relationships and lays firm foundations for children's emerging prosocial behaviour and self-efficacy. More challenging perhaps is enacting pedagogy that enables such playful relationships to develop.

Research across many disciplines and decades has shown that play appears to be the principal or leading way in which children explore and make sense of experience. Moreover, it is mainly enjoyable and meaningful to the player, and highly social (Carpendale and Lewis 2006). The value of play in human development and experience is beyond dispute but *how* precisely play contributes to human development is still open to debate (Smith 2010). There is widespread agreement that children play and explore naturally and spontaneously regardless of culture, place or time (Goncu and Gaskins 2007), and that play provides a powerful means through which they come to understand the complexities of the material, conceptual and social world. But while playing and exploring appear to be universal human drivers (Smith 2010), the extent to which such activities are encouraged or limited in children will be determined by specific cultural and social practices, shaped also by experiences of individual children in the home, through early attachments, relationships established with caregivers, and the nature of the communicative environment (Roulstone et al. 2011).

Playing and exploring in the EYFS

In England the importance of play and exploration is officially recognized in the most recent iteration of the EYFS (DfE 2012), the statutory framework for children from birth to school starting age at 5. The framework builds on a long-established tradition of play-based approaches to early years education in Western educational systems over more than two centuries. But increasingly in the past few decades as play has moved into the centre of the official regulatory context, so too have measures for assessment and accountability. It seems that play must have explicit value and purpose if it is to be part of children's early education. Pinning down precisely what that value is, is challenging to say the least, given that by definition play is notoriously difficult to measure and evaluate.

The EYFS states that:

> Each area of learning and development must be implemented through planned, purposeful play and through a mix of adult-led and child-initiated activity. Play is essential for children's development, building their confidence as they learn to explore, to think about problems, and relate to others. Children learn by leading their own play, and by taking part in play which is guided by adults.
>
> (DfE 2012)

There has been much debate in the early years sector about what 'planned, purposeful play' might look like and what the balance of adult-led and child-initiated activity should be. The EYFS gives little guidance on this, stating that 'There is an ongoing judgment to be made by practitioners about the balance between activities led by children, and activities led or guided by adults.'

Participating in children's play can be challenging for adults and this is especially true in play which contains high levels of fantasy. In this chapter I suggest that play provision needs to be planned carefully to ensure that children have access to a wide range of possibilities and opportunities, but as Brown (2009) suggests, if the purpose is more important than the act of play then it probably isn't play!

While the processes of 'playing and exploring' have been central to early years provision for many decades, its importance has been further reinforced as one of three key characteristics of effective learning in the EYFS. There is of course considerable overlap between the three areas and they should not be thought of as discrete types of learning. It is useful, however, to tackle each one separately as in the chapters of this book, to consider what is meant by, in this case, playing and exploring and the special ways in which these particular characteristics contribute to and provide the context for children's learning. That said, we should think in terms not only of the characteristics of *effective learning* but also of the characteristics of *effective pedagogy* and what these might mean for adults working with young children. I have suggested already that playful interactions with children are one powerful way to engage children. These characteristics are intended to provide the framework for engaging children's interest and emphasize the *process* and *context* rather than the content or outcomes of learning.

A sociocultural approach to play and exploration

This chapter is informed by a sociocultural approach to play and exploration, one which acknowledges the way in which learning and development are socially, as well as individually, constructed and where learner agency is central. The ideas of Vygotsky (1978) are particularly influential here. For Vygotsky, all learning and meaning is socially constructed during interaction and activity with others. From this perspective, children from birth are seen as active agents rather than passive recipients in the learning process. As we observe children, so they observe us and learn how to respond to achieve their goals, try to guess what is in our heads and work out what is acceptable and what is not. Babies search for meaning out of the array of experiences they encounter through heightened sensory engagement with the world, and through connecting socially with others. Even newborn babies actively signal a wide range of feelings such as discomfort, contentment or distress through bodily moves, non-verbal communication and by modifying behaviour according to the responses received. Older children learn how to resist adult requests and rules in order to meet their desires and needs, as when Zac (aged 4) says, 'the teacher decides if too many [in the play corner], unless the teacher's not looking'.

In this chapter 'agency' is understood as a person's way of being, seeing and responding in the world, as taking control of one's own mental activity within particular sociocultural contexts (Edwards 2001). There are, however, obvious limits to that agency, where children may not yet have the prerequisite skills to act on their ideas and decisions or where the structural features of early years settings such as rules, routines and regulations prevent them from doing so. In order for children to exercise agency they require adults that are able to recognize and work with those limits so that the adults do not come to dominate the child's experiences. This may require early years practitioners to rethink established ways of working and the traditional hierarchical relationship between adults and children, particularly in playful and exploratory situations. It is also possible that if we assume too much for children's agency that we fail to see the times when they need adult guidance, instruction and help in setting boundaries. Moreover, in the play between children, agency is not simply associated with the individual child, but is mediated by the interactions between children. Play offers children the opportunity to negotiate and contain their desire to act with other children, and thus to self-regulate behaviour and feeling. Through playing and exploring with adults, children can be encouraged to have an active role in shaping teaching and learning experiences in the early years setting. This might lead us to think of curriculum and pedagogy in the EYFS as co-constructed, a negotiated space, based on a reciprocal relationship between children and adults (Rogers 2010).

Play and exploration: the same or different?

James, aged 3.6 months, is building a 'marble run' with his dad. Together they connect the pieces that make the tower of intricate winding paths down which the marbles will eventually travel. Once the run is built, James releases marbles one by one through the chute, each one following the twists and turns with a clatter and rattle, settling eventually in the container at the bottom. James is clearly fascinated by the movement and the noise and repeats the action many times. Later he takes the box of some 25 marbles and releases all of them in quick succession, so that eventually some way down the run a marble 'jam' is created. When his dad tries to intervene to unblock the marbles, James is insistent that he wants to do this alone, without help and interference. He has deliberately created the marble jam and is fascinated by the long snake-like pattern that the marbles have created in the tube. James plays with the marble run for some 20 minutes before he is called away for supper, and he goes somewhat reluctantly. The marble run is packed away in his absence but later James asks for it several times and is clearly still preoccupied by it.

In this fairly typical activity that we might observe in the home or early years setting James demonstrates what Laevers (1993) describes as 'involvement':

- recognised by a child's concentration and persistence;
- characterised by motivation, fascination, an openness to stimuli and an intensity of experience both at the physical and cognitive level, and a deep satisfaction with a strong flow of energy;
- determined by the 'exploratory' drive and the child's individual developmental needs.

James clearly derives a great deal of pleasure and satisfaction from the activity, evident in the countless repetitions of the action of releasing the marbles. Yet he does not show this pleasure in any overt way, his facial expression remains serious and his gaze fixed on the task at hand. This is a good example of planned and purposeful play/exploration initiated and led by James. His dad played an important role too in helping him to set up the marble run and modelling what to do with the marbles initially. James's deliberate creation of the marble 'jam' suggests that he is interested in the potential of his actions, the 'what if' question that so often underpins playful and exploratory behaviours. His desire to take control of the activity and to resist the intervention from his dad to conform to the mundane and 'correct' use of the marble run is interesting because it reveals also the potential of materials to provoke not only exploratory behaviours but also the desire in young children to control the course of events and to commit to their ideas even in the face of adult alternatives. James was also exercising agency. When he is called away he showed displeasure and resistance but eventually complied when his dad intervened.

But is this play or exploration? And what can we learn from this example about the differences between play and exploration? If we think of this example as play, then we can conclude that play is very often serious and involves deep level engagement and concentration. James was completely absorbed in this solitary activity but it also appeared to include a strong sense of 'what if', a dialogue with the self: what will happen if I release all the marbles at once? Similar questions are suggested in play where children appear to try out and explore new roles: what if I pretend to be a monster? He shows that he is 'willing to have a go' (Early Education 2012) and keen to find out.

The terms play and exploration are often used interchangeably under the broader heading of 'play'. This ordinary and everyday example illustrates how distinguishing play from exploration is not straightforward. Indeed the coupling of 'playing and exploring' in the EYFS seems to suggest that there is much overlap between them. However, in the research literature an important distinction is sometimes made between play and exploration. The work of Hutt and colleagues (1989) is particularly significant in this area since it distinguished two distinct types of behaviour within the activity normally called 'play' and considered how these might relate to children's activity in early years settings. The research team observed the ways in which 3- to 5-year-olds responded to an unfamiliar toy and concluded that there were striking similarities in children's behaviour patterns. On the basis of this evidence, Hutt et al. suggested two main categories: exploration and play. Exploration involved the child in visual inspection, activity investigation and manipulation of the toy. According to the results, over a period of about six days the exploratory behaviour decreased and a new set of patterns of behaviours began to appear (Hutt et al. 1989: 4). They maintained that the child, having acquired information concerning the properties of the novel toy through 'exploration', now utilized that knowledge in what they termed 'play' and described the distinction in the following way: 'Implicit in the behaviours we termed "exploration" was the question: What does this *object* do?, whilst implicit in the behaviours we termed "play" was the question: What can *I* do with this object?' (1989: 4, original emphasis). This work suggests that exploration is more likely to occur when the child is faced with the unfamiliar and novel.

On the other hand, Hutt et al. (1989) suggest that play is more likely to occur when the child is faced with a familiar situation, event or object. In play children may draw on a wide range of prior knowledge, skills and concepts and these can be used in new and novel ways. Vygotsky wrote that in play 'a stick becomes a horse'. In other words, once the child is familiar with the properties of an object through exploration it can be used by the child in highly imaginative ways. In this example of role play in a reception class we see children 'playing with what they know' (Early Education 2012) drawing on a wide range of familiar everyday knowledge of objects, places and people in an imaginary context:

Roxanne: You can pretend to take an order but you're not the baby. [Runs out of the café and says 'can I have a piece of paper please to go in the café?']

Roxanne: Right what would you like madam? [pretending to write down the order].

Mia pretends to write it down and Roxanne interjects with 'I'm the person that writes it down and you're in the kitchen and gives it out.' Turning her attention back to her customer she asks 'right what would you like to drink madam?'

Sally: I would like a doughnut.

Mia: A doughnut.

Roxanne: No Mia don't tell her she doesn't know what there is . . . I'll tell her, there's water. Orange juice and ice-cream. Do you want any cereal? She wants an ice-cream' Gives the customer her 'food'.

Roxanne is now using the mobile phone (a brick) and pretends to write down an order. She says 'who's the mum, who's the mum? I'd like to have an order for some food but somebody's on the phone right as soon as we can.'

Roxanne to Mary 'somebody's rung up and they want 10 sausages, 10 glasses of milk and 10 ice-creams, they want it together, 'cos there's 10 of them all together'.

According to Hutt et al. (1989) play of the type illustrated above can be distinguished from the intense and concentrated observable behaviours typical of learning in a new situation or with a new material or object as in the example of James and the marble run activity. The distinction between exploration and play is, I think, a helpful one, if only because it enables us to think about the wide range of different behaviours we see in children's activities which we might call play. For babies and toddlers the emphasis appears to be on exploration through sensorimotor activity. For children in the 3 to 5 age group we tend to see a prevalence of pretend play. There may be good developmental reasons for this but it does not mean that babies and toddlers do not engage in playful behaviours and that exploration diminishes in older children. There is also a danger that the research by Hutt might give the rather misleading and inaccurate impression that exploration is more worthwhile than play since it appears to be linked more directly with the acquisition of new knowledge. The application of that new knowledge in the context of play is equally important and powerful and helps children to build their understanding of the world, to try things out in real and imaginary contexts and to communicate ideas and feelings to others. Drawing on Hutt's distinctions can help us to think through the range of possibilities available in materials and spaces made available to children. How often do we offer new and novel resources to children to stimulate exploratory knowledge-seeking behaviour? Do children have the opportunity to revisit materials so that they can re-use them in the context of their imaginary play once they have explored the physical and sensory properties of them? Do children have opportunities to play with open-ended materials?

It might be more helpful to think in terms of 'exploratory play', a term suggested by Hughes, as one possible kind of play that we might observe from many different types. Hughes developed a typology of 16 play types all of which are observable in early years settings. These are listed below but more detail can be found in Hughes (1996).

- exploratory play
- fantasy play
- imaginative play
- locomotive play
- object play
- role play
- symbolic play
- rough and tumble play
- socio-dramatic play
- social play
- creative play
- communication play
- dramatic play
- deep play

Exploratory play is described by Hughes as play 'to access factual information consisting of manipulative behaviours such as handling, throwing, banging or mouthing objects' but this may be accompanied by a playful disposition or combined with other types of play such as creative play or locomotive play. Perhaps the most important question to consider is how does naming an activity as play or exploration shape the ways in which adults respond to and support or limit children's experiences?

Exploratory competence and representational competence

Research suggests that to achieve play competence infants need to develop both exploratory and representational competence (Shore 1998; Campbell 2002). Exploratory competence is shown in children's visual attentiveness and object manipulation. Representational competence is the ability to use one thing (gesture, word or object) to stand for or represent something else and has obvious and strong links with later symbolic representation in the form of role play, language, mathematics and the arts. Through their pretend play, schemas and multi-modal activities, we can see how young children move from personal meaning-making to shared understandings of symbolic systems and build on this in the resources and experiences we provide. In the extracts above, James shows exploratory competence in the behaviours he displays when manipulating the marbles. Roxanne, by contrast, demonstrates representational competence when she uses a wooden brick as a mobile phone, and pretends to write a list. The development of both exploratory and representational competence depend on the support of parents and other adults, but that support is best given in the form of joint and reciprocal play. This happens, for example, in the home corner, when an adult takes turns to stir and taste the imaginary soup rather than simply hand over the spoon or ask the child questions about the realistic features of the soup (Campbell 2002). Entering into the imaginary world created by the child and engaging in joint play appears to lead to more extended play and language. Similarly, adults who offer babies and toddlers a 'secure base' from which to engage with an environment that stimulates exploratory activity can help children to become confident learners. For example, Goldschmied's work on treasure baskets and heuristic play, where the adult adopts the role of silent partner, 'provides young children with a secure base to venture from and playfully explore the environment, whilst the safe haven provides them with a refuge when that environment causes them any distress' (Rose and Rogers 2012: 35–6).

To become confident learners, children need to gain mastery of their environment through play and exploration. This might mean that they use materials in ways that adults have not considered, climb higher on the climbing frame than an adult might feel comfortable with and explore ideas that are challenging to adults such as death, violence and sex. But for children to achieve both representational and exploratory competence through play they need adults who allow for the sometimes messy outcomes of exploratory play and support children to take risks that give 'stretch' to their capabilities. It is through such play that young children are likely to develop a greater sense of self-worth and autonomy.

From playful beginnings: attachment and attunement

The ability to play and to respond to playful interactions from others is present from birth. In these early interactions lie the seeds of secure attachment and effective learning which cut across and influence all developmental domains. One of the earliest ways in which babies come to understand their place in the world is through the process of attachment to the primary caregiver, an idea initially suggested in the work of John Bowlby (1969). Attachment is a *relational* process where strong affectional ties are established between one person and another, most likely driven by a biological need for security and safety (Rose and Rogers 2012). In early years settings this role is taken by the key person, a role which has become a statutory requirement of the EYFS. Attachment can be established through playful interactions with newborns where the key person listens carefully to the sounds babies make in an effort to communicate with those around them. Adults also need to judge when babies do not feel playful. They may be tired, hungry or unwell. Or they may simply be overstimulated and uninterested. The outward signs of these mood states, visible in nonverbal and body language, provide important clues to the skilled early years practitioner, all of which are part of developing a playful pedagogy which ensures positive attachments are made.

Rose and Rogers (2012) state that secure attachment is achieved through adults being empathetically responsive (Underdown 2007), by looking closely for verbal and nonverbal signals from the child that reflect how the child is feeling and what their needs and interests might be. This is 'attunement', a term which refers to the deep, genuine and significant connection established with another human (typically but not exclusively with the primary caregiver). Attunement between baby and caregiver creates a context for reciprocal connectedness that powerfully influences the synaptic make-up of the brain and provides the foundation for learning and well-being.

In summary, according to Arredondo and Edwards (2000), attunement depends on the following key elements:

- emotional availability of the adult;
- high degree of flexibility from the adult;
- display of a range of affect (emotion);
- capacity for genuine playfulness;
- initiation of affectionate interactions;
- sense of humour;
- patience.

Once again we see that 'genuine playfulness' features in positive interactions with babies. Moreover it is through this early reciprocal play that the foundations are laid for babies to see that they exist in the world separately to other people. The feedback they receive from the caregiver is vitally important in affirming their place in the world and in encouraging subsequent attempts to communicate. The pleasure and affirmation that stem from these playful interactions encourage babies to repeat actions and sounds and to search out the caregiver.

The age of discovery! The case of heuristic play and treasure baskets (Goldschmied)

Exploratory play appears to be most prevalent in what Piaget described as the sensorimotor period typically from birth through to 2 years (1978). Babies try to make sense of the world in many ways - through grasping, sucking, banging and throwing objects. Through sensory and exploratory play, babies and young infants construct schemas, or 'patterns of repeatable actions that lead to early categories and then to logical classifications' (Athey 1990: 36). Building up a body of schemas through exploratory play enables children to learn about cause and effect, to test the properties of objects, and through their increasing mobility, to become spatially aware. In exploratory play, children rely on adults to provide an environment that affords interesting materials and objects for exploration and discovery, and also on interaction with and encouragement from other people. As babies are able to sit up and manipulate objects, the world takes on a different perspective and they gain greater independence in their play. A particular approach to sensorimotor play was developed by Elinor Goldschmied (1987), beginning with so-called 'treasure baskets' or collections of a range of everyday objects contained in a basket which provide multi-sensory experiences and encourage opportunities for hand/eye coordination (Rose and Rogers 2012). Goldschmied assigns the adult a passive rather than active role in heuristic play acting as a 'secure base' and 'safe haven' from which the child can explore. Child-led exploration allows for children's innate curiosity to flourish and supports their emerging sense of control and self-efficacy. Equally, however, adults might take a more proactive stance while children are exploring as Dowling suggests (2006). 'Scaffolding' children's learning through approaches such as 'sustained shared thinking' allows for a dialogue to develop centred on the activity. However, it is important not simply to ask questions about the properties of the objects – What colour is it? How many? Is it heavy? – but also to join in with modelling ways of exploring and affirming children's actions as in the example of James and his dad. Open-ended questions such as 'can you tell me how does it feel when you hold it?' or contributions such as 'I like the warm feeling of that, what do you think?' and 'I wonder what will happen if I put that on top?' are more beneficial to extending learning (Siraj-Blatchford and Manni 2008) whereas closed questions when overused may shut down possibilities for exploratory and playful behaviours. Knowing when to step back and allow the child to explore alone is important too.

From these early explorations and playful interactions, babies begin to build a bank of experiences and associated images from which they come to make sense of the world around them. Although research is unclear about the precise age at which babies begin to hold onto mental representations, the ability is certainly present in infants from around 5 months. We call this *object permanence* or, put simply, the ability to remember something that is no longer present. This ability to hold images in our head is a uniquely human achievement. Imagine if we couldn't do this. Of course, you couldn't imagine at all without this powerful capacity for remembering or for mental representation. Remembering something that is absent in this way is quite distinct from recognition of something when it is present. These mental representations enable children to remember and recall images of familiar people or things even in their absence. Without this capacity children would not be able to develop imitative and pretend play. However, a second capacity which develops in the second year of life enables children to move beyond mental representations to more complex, social imaginative activity. This is the development of a 'theory of mind'.

Developing a theory of mind in the context of play

Developing a theory of mind, that is, knowing that someone else thinks differently from you, is a vital human skill which has particular relevance for the ability of children to engage in play, and particularly pretend play. As we saw in the example of Roxanne and the café, being in role, acting out the thoughts and feelings of others, and negotiating role-play plots all require that children understand perspectives and experiences different from their own. Shared pretence, then, may be a particularly significant spur for the development and consolidation of theory of mind skills (Dunn 2004). As far as we know, babies in the first year of life do not engage in pretend play (Gopnik et al. 1999). In the second year of life we see the emergence of imitative behaviours and early pretence. For example, at 18 months Laura imitates her mother by 'combing' her hair with a comb she finds on a table. Later at 24 months Laura is playing 'mums and babies' with her sister, Kara, aged 4. Laura pretends to comb her hair with a wooden brick that she finds in the toy box. She shows that she can substitute one thing for another, a vital skill in the development of symbolic thought, which provides the foundation for later learning across all subjects. This type of play develops rapidly over the next few years and becomes increasingly elaborate and varied. Between the ages of about 3 and 5 we see significant changes in the nature and quality of pretend play as children begin to organize and assign roles to others as well as adopt roles themselves. Their play becomes increasingly social and complex.

Key points to consider in the development of play and exploration include:

- Play helps children to develop a sense of self and the world around them and appears to be linked to the development of theory of mind.

- Through playful interactions and exploration babies and young children begin to build up a mental model of themselves as separate from others.

- Children's emerging sense of self is enhanced or reduced by the feedback the young child receives from those around them.

- Object permanence and theory of mind skills are essential to the growth of imagination, play and problem solving.

- Children aged 24 months–5 years engage in more social pretend play than any other kind of play!

- Social pretend play between children builds social, communication and intellectual skills.

- The ability to move beyond the here and now, between belief and make-believe, is a uniquely human activity.

- Children aged 3–5 engage in more pretend play than any other form of play.

- From about the age of 4, children begin to assign roles as well as adopt roles.

- Children from around 3–5 have a strong desire to self-generate themes in play.

Outdoor play, rules and risk taking

It is Sabina's first day at nursery. She is wearing a beautiful velvet dress with matching slippers. Her mum is with her helping her to settle in. Together they move to the outdoor area. A group of children are playing around a large 'puddle' into which water from a pump overflows. One child is pouring water into the puddle from a can. Another is pumping the water, while another is wearing wellington boots and runs through the puddle splashing and laughing. The nursery teacher is talking quietly to the children about what they are doing. Sabina watches for a while then runs through the puddle with obvious pleasure. She is still wearing her velvet slippers.

What is interesting about this brief observation is the reaction of the adults. We might have expected Sabina's mother or the teacher to have tried to stop her or reacted loudly or even reprimanded her. Instead, the teacher calmly suggested that Sabina might like to come inside and find some boots. It was the experience that was important at that moment and of course, the slippers could be dried out. So often we curtail children's explorations because concerns over mess, safety and noise take precedence. In so doing we might actually discourage children from 'having a go' (Early Education 2012).

The outdoors offers a range of different learning opportunities and characteristics to the indoors not least because it offers children freedom to be more active, noisy and exploratory than is possible in indoor spaces. In addition to the obvious physical benefits of being in the outdoors, such activity offers young children a range of multi-sensory, first-hand experiences such as feeling the effects of the weather and related temperatures, coming into direct contact with the textures and smells of natural materials such as grass, ice, earth, water and wood, as in the case of Sabina. Grassy banks, garden areas, walls, fences and tarmac surfaces provide an interesting array of features, textures and mini environments for children to explore. A small grassy hill or a few shrubs can be transformed into mountains and forests as children play (Rogers and Evans 2008). Open-ended resources such as large boxes, drapes and large construction materials encourage children to create imaginary worlds and develop complex narratives. The EYFS (DfE 2012) promotes the view that the outdoors has equal value to the indoor classroom and that, where possible, children should be able to move seamlessly between the two environments, in what we call 'free flow' play. Such play enables children to combine elements of indoor and outdoor learning, to mix resources in creative and innovative ways and develop a sense of place and space. Young children need to create and explore their own places through the use of open-ended and suggestive (rather than overly prescriptive), props and materials and there are obvious limitations to what is possible indoors, in terms of space, noise level and the nature of the resources. The outdoor environment allows children to play on a larger scale and to explore a wider range of resources.

Much of what has been said about playing and exploring in this chapter applies to the outdoor environment and in particular the need for adults to interact in ways which allow children to take the lead and which foster confidence and enjoyment. But there are also different challenges inherent in outdoor spaces. Play and exploration, particularly in outdoor spaces, by their very nature involve children taking risks which push them beyond their current capabilities and challenge them physically, socially and cognitively. For adults, managing risk is challenging too and may lead to anxieties about how far they can allow children to explore and push boundaries. Certain types of play can also pose a risk to adults' own boundaries about what is acceptable behaviour, particularly within the heavily regulated classroom. This is why we see differing levels of tolerance of physical, noisy play in indoor and outdoor spaces (Waite et al. 2011). As children develop they move from a situation of dependence and adult-managed experiences to independence and self-management. Gill (2006) argues that there is growing evidence to suggest that in the developed Western world an increasingly regulated, risk averse approach is severely limiting children's opportunities to practise some of the vital skills that would enable them to make this move and to exercise good judgement about what constitutes risk and danger. Recent research by Waite et al. (2011) notes that adults in early years settings may hold an exaggerated view of what constitutes a risk to young children, stemming from their own personal anxiety about potentially threatening situations, about the potential for disorder within the group and a genuine anxiety about litigation while *in loco parentis*. Clearly the views held by adults will strongly influence the nature of provision and the extent to which children have licence to explore their environment. Indeed several research studies confirm that opportunities afforded to children to take risks are highly dependent on how risk is viewed by adults (Stephenson 2003; Waters and Begley 2007; Waite et al. 2011). A study of practitioner beliefs about risk in play in Australia and Norway (Little et al. 2012) demonstrated that where there were shared views on the benefits of risk and in how risk was understood, there were significant differences between the countries in how risk was enacted in practice. Perhaps unsurprisingly, the Australian educators felt more constrained by the regulatory and pedagogical context that arose from it. By contrast the regulatory environment in which the Norwegian practitioners operated provided greater flexibility, allowing these practitioners to exercise their own professional judgement to manage children's risky play.

For some adults, the pedagogic challenge may stem from their personal attitude towards the outdoors. Inclement weather conditions and the often physical, risky and boisterous nature of outdoor play can be off-putting for some adults. Adult attitudes to outdoor play may also be gendered, expecting and encouraging more physical and messy play for boys than girls (Tovey 2010). Adults may perceive that girls are in need of greater protection outdoors from potential threats such as accidents, bad weather and strangers. The study of outdoor learning in Foundation Stage and Year 1 classes by Waite et al. (2011) found that the dominant form of interaction in the outdoor areas was for the purpose of preventing risk through admonishment or curtailing children's activity. How can we ensure that young children have ample opportunities to take risks and maximize the impact of the outdoor learning environment?

Tovey (2010) suggests that rather than emphasize risk assessment, we need to embrace risk as an essential part of play pedagogy. In keeping with the overriding message in this chapter, children need time, space and flexible resources to develop outdoor play that allows for risk-taking but so that it does not become the main or leading focus of planning for the outdoor play. Playing and Exploring in the EYFS promotes the view that that children should have opportunities to

- initiate activities
- seek challenge

- show a can do attitude
- take a risk, engaging in new experiences and learning by trial and error.

Outdoor spaces offer children freedom to explore and test out their capabilities, which often exceed our expectations. But to achieve this children need adults who enjoy the outdoors and understand the wide-ranging benefits it brings.

Valuing children's play and exploration

This chapter has emphasized the importance of establishing playful relationships with babies and young children to help establish positive feelings about learning and to encourage them to explore the world with increasing autonomy, confidence and feelings of self-worth. As children approach the end of the EYFS and 'school readiness' becomes more pressing, it is easy to view play instrumentally, as a vehicle through which to deliver the prescribed curriculum and assess the concepts, skills and knowledge children have acquired. This may mean that the type of free flow, flexible play that we see in nursery settings where children have extended periods to choose play partners, resources and spaces, is increasingly interrupted by the demands of more formal learning activities such as phonics and reading with an adult. To illustrate, consider the following example observed in a reception class:

Chris, Hannah and Molly are playing in the 'hospital'. After some persuasion from Molly, Chris agrees to lie down and becomes the 'patient'. At the same time he is called away by an adult to 'change his books':

Molly: There's no patient in yet he's just changing his books.

Chris is clearly reluctant to leave the role-play area, and hesitates. Then he complies with the adult's request. However, while reading to the adult, he repositions the barrier around the role-play area. With one foot in the role-play area and the other foot outside Chris is 'balancing' both tasks.

Rhia approaches the hospital and Chris, anxious to stay in the play, immediately interjects 'you can't go in there, 'cos I'm the patient!'

On Chris's return Molly is called away to undertake another activity and she says to Rhia 'don't let anyone in 'cos I've got to go somewhere.'

Hannah is then called away to do her book bag. As she leaves she says to Rhia 'don't let anyone else in here.' Eliza arrives in the area and sits down at the computer. As agreed with Hannah,

Rhia says: 'Eliza you can't go there 'cos Hannah's playing.'

The many interruptions in this short episode of play meant that little time was spent in developing the role-play narrative. On the surface, the pedagogy in this classroom appeared to be play based. However, closer observation showed that pedagogy emphasized 'school readiness' and teacher-led activity; play in this example is functioning as a holding task rather than an activity valued as an important context for children's learning. The EYFS is clear that adults need to 'ensure children have uninterrupted time to play and explore' and this is as important for children in reception classes as it is for their nursery peers.

Transition from EYFS to Year 1 is potentially challenging for both children and adults as children move from active to more passive modes of learning and from child-led to adult-led learning experiences. Many children look forward to school and the status that can bring. Some will be ready for more passive types of learning. Others will need time to adapt to new ways of working and learning. Starting school should not be the end of playing and exploring but inevitably there will be fewer opportunities in the classroom for the kinds of activities enjoyed in early years settings. Ideally, Key Stage 1 classrooms will continue to offer active, playful and exploratory experiences to children and also allow regular access to the outdoors. Such an approach will help smooth the transition and allow children to build on the firm foundations established in the EYFS. To conclude this chapter I offer a few points for reflection. Playing and exploring are vital to young children from birth. Few would dispute this view. But how can we best support the unpredictable, messy, noisy and potentially risky elements that arise in the context of play and exploration that are challenging for adults? Sometimes it means putting to one side our own attitudes and assumptions and shifting the focus to what is important – as in the case of Sabina and the velvet slippers. In terms of developing a pedagogy which supports play and exploration it means:

- giving children real choice about where, with whom, what and how they play;
- providing flexible spaces (indoors and outdoors) and *uninterrupted* time to play, to revisit, rebuild and recreate ideas with adults and children;
- tuning into and following children's ideas;
- showing children we are interested in their play through playful interactions, co-construction, consultation and negotiation, observation and feedback;
- being knowledgeable others and advocates for play and exploration.

References

Arredondo, D. and Edwards, L.P. (2000) Attachment, bonding and reciprocal connectedness, *Journal for the Center for Families, Children and the Courts*, 1: 109–27.
Athey, C. (1990) *Extending Thought in Young Children*. London: Paul Chapman.

Bornstein, M., Haynes, M., Watson, A. and Painter, K., (1996) Solitary and collaborative pretense play in early childhood: sources of individual variation in the development of representational competence, *Child Development*, 67(6): 2910–29.

Bowlby, J. (1969) *Attachment and Loss. Vol. 1: Attachment.* New York: Basic Books.

Brown, S. (2009) *Play: How it Shapes the Brain, Opens the Imagination and Invigorates the Soul.* New York: Penguin.

Campbell, S. (2002) *Behaviour Problems in Pre-school Children: Clinical and Developmental Issues.* New York: Guilford Press.

Carpendale, J. and Lewis, C. (2006) *How Children Develop Social Understanding.* Oxford: Wiley-Blackwell.

DfE (Department for Education) (2012) *Statutory Framework for the Early Years Foundation Stage: Setting the Standards for Learning, Development and Care for Children from Birth to Five.* www.foundationyears.org.uk/early-years-foundation-stage-2012/ or http://www.education.gov.uk/aboutdfe/statutory/g00213120/eyfs-statutory-framework (accessed 1 January 2013).

Dowling, M. (2006) *Supporting Young Children's Sustained Shared Thinking: Training Materials.* London: Early Education (The British Association for Early Childhood Education).

Dunn, J. (2004) *Children's Friendships: The Beginnings of Intimacy.* Oxford: Wiley-Blackwell.

Early Education (2012) *Development Matters in the Early Years Foundation Stage.* London: Early Education. www.early-education.org.uk and for download at www.foundationyears.org.uk/early-years-foundation-stage-2012/ (accessed 20 December 2012).

Edwards, A. (2001) Researching pedagogy: a sociocultural agenda, *Pedagogy, Culture and Society*, 9(2): 161–86.

Gill, R. (2006) *The Theory and Practice of Leadership.* London: Sage.

Goldschmied, E. (1987) *Infants at Work.* VHS video. London: National Children's Bureau.

Goncu, A., and Gaskins, S. (eds) (2007) *Play and Development: Evolutionary, Sociocultural and Functional Perspectives.* Mahwah, NJ: Lawrence Erlbaum Associates.

Gopnik, A., Meltzoff, A. and Kuhl, P. (1999) *How Babies Think.* London: Weidenfeld and Nicolson.

Hughes, B. (1996) *A Playworker's Taxonomy of Play Types.* London: Playlink.

Hutt, S., Hutt, C., Tyler, S. and Christopherson, H. (1989) *Play, Exploration and Learning: A Natural History of the Pre-school.* London: Routledge.

Laevers, F. (1993) Deep-level learning, an exemplary application on the area of physical knowledge, *European Early Childhood Education Research Journal*, 1(1): 53–68.

Little, H., Sandseter, E. and Wyver, A. (2012) Early childhood teachers' beliefs about children's risky play in Australia and Norway, *Contemporary Issues in Early Childhood*, 13(4): 300–16.

Parker-Rees, R. (2007) Liking to be liked: imitation, familiarity and pedagogy in the first years of life, *Early Years*, 27(1): 3–17.

Piaget, J. (1978) *The Development of Thought.* Oxford: Blackwell.

Rogers, S. (2010) Powerful pedagogies and playful resistance: researching children's perspectives, in E. Brooker and S. Edwards (eds) *Engaging Play.* Maidenhead: Open University Press.

Rogers, S. and Evans, J. (2008) *Inside Role-play in Early Education.* London: Routledge.

Rose, J. and Rogers, S. (2012) *Adult Roles in the Early Years.* Maidenhead: Open University Press.

Roulstone, S., Law, J., Rush, R., Clegg, J. and Peters, T. (2011) *Investigating the Role of Language in Children's Early Educational Outcomes,* DFE Research Report DFE-RR134. http//www.education.gov.uk/publications/eOrderingDownload/DFE-RR134.pdf (accessed December 2012).

Shore, C. (1998) Play and language: individual differences as evidence of development and style, in D. Fromberg and D. Bergen (eds) *Play from Birth to Twelve: Contexts, Perspectives and Meanings.* New York: Garland Publishing.

Siraj-Blatchford, I. and Manni, L. (2008) 'Would you like to tidy up now?' An analysis of adult questioning in the English Foundation Stage, *Early Years,* 28(1): 5–22.

Smith, P.K. (2010) *Children and Play.* Oxford: Wiley-Blackwell.

Stephenson, A. (2003) Physical risk-taking: dangerous or endangered?' *Early Years,* 23(1): 35–43.

Tovey, H. (2010) Playing on the edge: perceptions of risk and danger in outdoor play, in P. Broadhead, J. Howard and E. Wood (eds) *Play and Learning in the Early Years.* London: Sage.

Underdown, A. (2007) *Young Children's Health and Well-being.* Maidenhead: Open University Press.

Vygtosky, L. (1978) *Mind in Society: The Development of Higher Psychological Processes.* Cambridge, MA: Harvard University Press.

Waite, S., Rogers, S. and Evans, J. (2011) A time of change: outdoor learning and pedagogies of transition between Foundation Stage and Year 1, in S. Waite (ed.) *Children Learning Outside the Classroom.* London: Sage.

Waters, J. and Begley, S. (2007) Supporting the development of risk-taking behaviours in the early years: an exploratory study, *Education 3–13,* 35(4): 365–77.

4 Active learning

Nancy Stewart

Introduction

The most effective learning involves energy and commitment from the learner. Children learn as they interact with people and things, but while they may not recognize this as learning at the time, this does not mean they are passively and unconsciously soaking up knowledge and understanding. Central to working with the characteristics of effective learning is the understanding that children, as the agents of their own learning, must be willing to actively expend mental and physical effort in the process.

Adults may be skilful at providing opportunities and supporting children to learn, but learning can never be done for another person. This chapter is about how children actively conduct their own learning. Learning theories have moved beyond the transmission model of teaching and learning which assumes knowledge and understanding can be directly transferred from the more knowledgeable person. Instead, social constructivist theory explains that while a more expert partner opens doors to new possibilities and supports use of these new approaches, the learner must actually do the work of mentally interpreting and linking the new input to existing understandings. This may involve building new concepts or restructuring existing understanding as required to make the learning usable for the individual. The learner, then, is not a passive recipient of their learning but is the active agent in the process.

The active part children play in their learning goes far beyond the physical activity which is a natural element of being a young child. Moving and physically experiencing the world are prime sources of gathering information and of stretching competence, independence and understanding. The term 'active learning' is sometimes used in this sense: children learn by doing, and so learning opportunities should be hands-on and involve concrete materials and movement rather than passive, abstract experiences. In terms of the characteristics of effective learning, however, the focus on hands-on physical experience sits more clearly within the strand of playing and exploring.

Engaging in experiences through movement and the senses is an essential part of children's learning and development – but it is not enough. The three characteristics of effective learning in the EYFS can be described as 'ready, willing and able'. Children playing and exploring are having the experiences that give the raw material for them to learn from; they are ready to learn. They must also be willing (active learning) and able (creating and thinking critically).

It is possible for children to be 'hands-on, brains-off'. A newspaper report on a newly opened interactive museum display described children's use of the buttons and flashing lights: 'Children flit; they see a button, press it and move on to the next, without pausing to reflect on what has happened. It just becomes a button-pressing experience rather than true interactive learning' (Hall 1995). Children may move so quickly between activities that the possibilities for learning are limited. They can also be physically active in ways which are routine and repetitive without bringing real discovery or thought to bear.

Lilian Katz (2000: 394) draws a clear distinction between shallow engagement and the quality of involvement that leads to learning:

> Take care not to confuse what is exciting, amusing, and fun with what is educative. Excitement is appropriate for entertainment and special occasions; it is short-lived pleasure – easy come, easy go. But what is educative requires sustained effort and involvement, often includes many routine elements, and offers long-term deep satisfaction rather than momentary fun and excitement.

To be an effective learner requires more than superficial engagement in an experience. It requires becoming involved and concentrating, expending effort and persevering with an activity even when it is difficult or not turning out to plan. This active involvement is driven by the desire to satisfy a goal, whether the goal at the time is experiencing competence in the activity or building understanding. 'Active learning' in this chapter, then, refers not primarily to physical engagement but to the way the learner is actively committed to the learning process. In other words, the child has the will – the motivation – to expend energy and effort to learn.

Motivation

Motivation can be considered to be the driving force that both propels and maintains interest and engagement towards achieving a goal. Martha Bronson (2000: 5) outlines the importance of motivation for self-regulating learners:

> It gets physical, social, and cognitive activities started and keeps them going by providing both the direction or goal for action and the force necessary to sustain effort. Motivation is at the centre of self-regulation and must be considered in relation to the development of all forms of voluntary control.

Developing the will to strive towards personal goals has a resounding life-long impact, and is linked to achieving success in learning as well as other endeavours. Of course, people do not maintain a uniform level of motivation towards all activities – we are all much more highly motivated to do some things than others, and we become more particular about where we aim our motivation as we grow older. An orientation to motivation, however, does seem to be something that is developed in the early years as children develop attitudes and habits of mind which carry through into their later experiences. Motivation in childhood has been found to predict motivation and success later in life, and while not uniform across areas of endeavour there remains a more generalized level of motivation (Lai 2011: 14). It may be that motivation becomes an approach to experience that children develop and carry with them over time and across contexts such as home, school, or in relationships (Grolnick et al. 1999: 3–14).

Early years practitioners who understand the importance of children's motivation will be concerned to identify what this quality of active learning looks like in action, and what their role is in protecting and fostering children's natural motivation to learn. When helping children to be strong learners is a clear goal of the adult, this will help to guide decisions about why, whether, when and how to intervene and interact with children in their learning.

Sources of motivation

The amount of effort and persistence the youngest children bring to their experiences is phenomenal, and results in enormous amounts of learning in the first years of life that we never again match as we grow older. From helpless infants who are encountering the world of time, space, objects and other people for the first time, children push themselves to attempt, to practise and to master physical skills, communication with others, and understanding what things are and how things work. What is it that pushes babies to learn? And how can we build on that natural impetus to support children to remain strong and committed learners, and avoid giving negative messages that risk shutting down learning capacity?

Self-determination theorists propose that innate needs, part of the inborn psychological nature of human beings, lie are at the root of motivation. These are described as the need to feel *competent*, to have *autonomy*, and to be *related to others* (Deci and Ryan 1985).

It is easy to see how the need for feeling competent to manage our world and our lives would support us to master new skills and build understanding, from egging a baby on to take up new challenges to spurring us on to further learning at any stage. Adults who support children's need for competence provide stimulation in both relationships and environments, provoking children to engage with the next challenge on their horizon.

The need for autonomy, or being in control of our own decisions and actions, is concerned with needing to feel that we are agents in our own lives and not simply passive recipients of what life brings. The more children have autonomous experiences where they are aware that they are making choices and making things happen in their world, the more they will repeat and seek out those satisfying experiences. From the baby who is able to see a toy move in response when they wave their hands or who knows they can elicit a response from an adult in response to their noises, to an older child who makes choices about their activities and is encouraged to do things in their own ways, children who know they have autonomy play an active part in their learning. They avoid the demotivation of learned helplessness, where a lack of opportunity to exercise autonomy results in the belief that nothing they can do makes any difference.

The need for warm, caring relationships with others is fundamental to being human, and is well recognized in theories of attachment for its emotional impact as well as its impact on development and learning. The relational and emotional aspects of motivation come into play in determining whether children feel safe and secure enough to explore, to take risks, and have the emotional resilience to bounce back from setbacks. The need for relationships – for a sense of belonging – also motivates children to take part in the social interactions that enable them to co-construct their understanding, and to begin to identify with and be motivated towards the goals of those with whom they connect.

The desire to satisfy these innate psychological needs arises within the learner, and so can be seen as an internal source of motivation – leading to *intrinsic motivation*. There are other sources of intrinsic motivation, as well, including the person feeling interest or curiosity and enjoyment in the experience itself. Deci and Ryan propose that interest and enjoyment are intrinsic motivators, as long as the essential underlying needs for competence, autonomy and relatedness are satisfied within the activity. If the experience denies satisfaction of these needs, however, then interest alone will not maintain motivation. It is as if competence, autonomy and relatedness are basic necessary nutrients for psychological development, as food is for life and physical growth. We will follow interesting pursuits when we are not hungry, but if we are starving we soon lose interest in anything but the need for food. Their definition of intrinsically motivated behaviours is 'those that are freely engaged out of interest without the necessity of separable consequences, and, to be maintained, they require satisfaction of the needs for autonomy and competence' (Deci and Ryan 2000: 233).

Intrinsic motivation, which arises from within the individual and where the activity itself brings satisfaction, can be seen in contrast to *extrinsic motivation*, which relates to behaviour arising from factors outside the person and outside the behaviour itself. Behaviourist theory holds that development and learning occur primarily in response to factors from outside of the individual. Some of these external factors are described as positive or negative reinforcements, where behaviour is more likely to be repeated if it is met with a reinforcement. A positive reinforcement occurs when a child learns that something good happens when they do a certain behaviour (such as people giving pleasant attention when a baby smiles), and a negative reinforcement is learning that something unpleasant stops in response to a behaviour (for example, being left alone in your cot will stop when you cry for attention). These reinforcers are consequences of the behaviour, and are quite different from rewards and punishments that occur not as a natural consequence, but are administered by someone else and are separate from the activity itself.

Children certainly can and do learn behaviours through reinforcements, and their ability to make the association between their behaviour and the reinforcement or external rewards can be used to shape behaviours that are seen as desirable. This is, however, an essentially passive view of children's development and learning – with children simply noticing the patterns between what they do and the response, and passively receiving the set of reinforcers that is available to them. It certainly cannot account for the enormous explosion of learning that young children engage in.

While there are both intrinsic and extrinsic sources of motivation, for children to become self-regulating learners there are significant advantages in supporting an orientation to intrinsic motivation. Intrinsic motivation is associated with higher achievement, welcoming challenge, becoming more involved in learning, using strategies more effectively, greater persistence and developing deeper understanding that can be applied across situations. When external motivation causes someone to take on an activity not for its own sake but in order to gain an unrelated reward, the person does not bring the energizing focus of interest, curiosity and enjoyment, nor commitment to the activity itself. Instead the focus is on the reward, so that doing just enough to get by can be substituted for doing all that the person has the potential to do. 'Intrinsic motivation has emerged as an important phenomena (sic) for educators – a natural wellspring of learning and achievement that can be systematically catalyzed or undermined by parent and teacher practices' according to Ryan and Stiller (1991: 115–49). Exploring how early years practice can support children as active learners will require attention to maintaining that vital wellspring.

Goal orientation – mastery or performance?

Motivation is not a generalized feeling, but always has a direction towards a goal. The type of goal someone sets strongly affects how they approach their activities, and researchers have identified the qualities and effects of two basic categories of goal: *mastery goals* and *performance goals*. Mastery goals are sometimes called 'learning goals', because the person's goal is to increase their competence to the best of their ability. Success is seen within the personal *process* of improvement. With performance goals, on the other hand, the person wants to show their competence to a standard relative to other people, with the end *product* determining success. In a sense, a mastery goal is never reached because we can always learn more, and this orientation pulls the learner forward to achieve more in the long term. A performance goal, however, is short term and may be met even when it is not stretching for the individual – performance can be 'good enough' to get by without the person reaching their potential. In fact, you may prefer to manage an easy task that will make you look good rather than take the risk of failing on a more challenging task.

There are many other advantages to mastery goals. People with a mastery goal focus on the task, while those with a performance goal focus on their self-image and are distracted by measuring how well they are doing compared to others. Those who hold a mastery goal are more likely to become more deeply involved in their activities, using deep processing so that they are able to truly own the learning, while a performance goal means one is more likely to engage just on the surface of the task. People with a mastery orientation are more likely to persevere in the face of difficulty, interpreting failure in terms of not having made enough effort and so responding by trying harder (Ames and Archer 1988: 260–7). Performance-oriented people are less likely to persevere because they tend to respond to failure by assuming they lack the ability, and so feel helpless to do anything about it (Dweck and Leggett 1988: 256–73).

Interestingly, people with a mastery orientation have greater access to an important source of learning – collaborating with other people. Co-constructing knowledge and understanding through working together and sustained shared thinking with peers is an important arena for children's learning, and the skill of collaboration remains critical for success in adult occupations and is highly valued by employers. People with a mastery orientation readily share ideas and work together with others, because their focus is on quality of learning in the task. Performance-oriented people, however, are competing with others, want to be seen to be right and as more competent than others, and so do not readily explore ideas together (Darnon et al. 2006).

The links between the type of goal and intrinsic and extrinsic motivation are clear: mastery goals are pursued with intrinsic motivation towards the internal satisfaction of increased competence, while performance goals are pursued for extrinsic reward such as a certain ranking, mark or praise. While recent and current research demonstrates the limiting nature of performance goals and extrinsic rewards compared to a mastery orientation, Ruedy and Nirenberg (1990: 238) quote the ancient Chinese sage Chuang Tzu who described the difference thousands of years ago:

> **The Need to Win**
> When an archer is shooting for nothing
> He has all his skill.
> If he shoots for a brass buckle
> He is already nervous.
> If he shoots for a prize of gold
> He goes blind

> Or sees two targets -
> He goes out of his mind!
> His skill has not changed. But the prize
> Divides him. He cares.
> He thinks more of winning
> Than of shooting -
> And the need to win
> Drains him of power.

Retaining children's power to learn must be a central goal of early education, and using external motivators and focusing on the end result rather than the process risks distracting children from their powerful internal drives to learn.

Growth and fixed mindsets

One way to describe the cluster of motivational attitudes and approaches that support learning power is the concept of a growth mindset, developed by researcher Carol Dweck (Dweck 2006). Through her research with children as young as 4, Dweck has identified a belief held by some people that intelligence and ability are not fixed, but grow through effort and practice. This growth mindset leads to a mastery orientation, to welcoming and enjoying challenges as an opportunity to improve, and to facing difficulty by using greater effort or changing strategy.

The opposite is a fixed mindset, characterized by the belief that intelligence and ability are fixed and cannot be changed. According to this mindset, an individual may or may not have particular talents and abilities – finding a task easy to do indicates that they happen to be good at it, while if it is difficult this means they are not good at it. The fixed mindset leads to people avoiding challenges which might prove difficult and so give uncomfortable messages about a lack of ability, preferring to repeat the same level of unchallenging tasks. The person with a fixed mindset experiences a sense of helplessness in the face of challenge and believes there is nothing they can do to deal with the obstacle. This feeling of a lack of autonomy, of having no power in the situation, is enough to turn someone with a fixed mindset away from potential learning opportunities.

Where do different mindsets come from? Dweck and her colleagues have identified the effect of subtle messages adults give to children which result in either a growth or a fixed mindset. In their experiments, when children succeed at a relatively easy puzzle task and are praised for their effort (that is, the active role they took in their success) they then show a growth mindset; they attribute difficulties with harder puzzles to needing more effort, and they are interested to work with more challenging puzzles. But when the children are praised for their ability to solve the easy puzzles ('you must be really good at these' – that is, the passive role of happening to have that ability) they then show a fixed mindset, and interpret not succeeding with harder puzzles to mean that they are not good at puzzles after all. They choose not to try harder puzzles, but to return to the easy level where they can expect success. Dweck has found evidence of growth or fixed mindsets in children as young as age 4, and has identified links between the type of praise parents give their children between ages 1 and 3 with their mindset and desire for challenge five years later.

'Active learning' in the characteristics of effective learning in the EYFS is outlined in three strands:

- being involved and concentrating;
- keeping trying;
- enjoying achieving what they set out to do.

These describe the way children are motivated agents in their learning, and each can be enhanced by skilful and sensitive adults through their interactions with children and through providing an environment geared to learning.

Being involved and concentrating

Children may show interest in an activity or a phenomenon for any number of reasons. It may be simply a novelty that attracts attention for a brief exploration, with initial interest being easily satisfied. Or perhaps the activity is simply fun – it may offer a wonderful feeling of stretching physical capacities, or be pleasurable for its sensual qualities, or be enjoyable and rewarding for its social involvement with others. Perhaps it is satisfying because involves repeating a familiar activity or skill, which brings a sense of security or confidence in having mastery.

A brief and superficial interest, however, is unlikely to lead to learning that takes the child to new levels of understanding. Deep learning results when the learner explores and tests many facets of the experience, relating the experience to previous understanding and building the robust mental links that allow them to use the new information, applying it in new situations. This focused attention and energy is what is meant by involvement and concentration.

Concentration versus development of attention

Babies and young children are sometimes described as being unable to concentrate, but nothing could be further from the truth. The degree of focus and sustained attention even quite young babies can bring to an object of interest can be striking to a quiet observer. There is, however, a developmental element to attention, with neurological maturation gradually enabling children more purposefully to control their attention.

A young baby will be immediately distracted by a more dominant stimulus – so talking to the concentrating baby can end the period of attention to the object of their interest. Gradually children develop the ability to resist distractions, but still need to pay attention to one thing at a time and cannot easily shift their attention at will. Eventually children become able to shift attention from one focus to another and back again, to pay attention to more than one thing at the same time, and finally to purposefully maintain focus for brief periods on something that is not of their own choosing.

Since children can concentrate on and become deeply involved in the experiences that they feel drawn to long before they can concentrate at will on something of someone else's choice, it is important to recognize that children choosing their own focus of learning is an important element of their will to learn.

Involvement in learning

Involvement in learning is rooted in true curiosity, which brings together an initial arousal of interest in something new with a deeper need to understand. Piaget's theories of assimilation and accommodation describe cognitive development as a response to taking in new information that may not fit with existing mental structures – our current hypotheses about what is and how things work. That cognitive dissonance is uncomfortable, and causes us to try to resolve the inconsistency by seeking more information. We investigate to find out whether we can after all assimilate the new phenomenon into what we already understand, or whether we will need to shift our mental map to fit the new information. For people to show real curiosity leading to sustained involvement they must be both open to something new and determined to understand – in other words, have the clear mastery goal of increasing knowledge.

Ferre Laevers, whose Leuven scale for involvement offers a clear way to observe the quality of children's involvement in their activity, has described the importance of children learning through deep involvement: 'Nurturing the learner's exploratory drive is critical as it can lead to lifelong learning . . . The aim is to encourage deep-level learning as opposed to superficial learning that does not affect the basic competencies and has little transfer to real life situations' (Laevers 1993: 53–68). The involvement signals are useful indicators of intense mental activity which indicates learning and development is taking place. Laevers identifies observable signals including the child's concentration, energy, creativity, facial expression and posture, persistence, precision, reaction time, language and satisfaction. These can be observed in children of any age in any context, and are interpreted according to descriptors of five levels from extremely low to extremely high involvement. This provides a tool for understanding and reflecting on practice and provision for a group as a whole, and for identifying individual children who demonstrate lower levels of involvement with the aim of considering what could be done to support greater involvement.

Laevers (2005: 4) describes involvement as

> strong motivation, fascination and total implication; there is no distance between person and activity, no calculation of possible benefits . . . The crucial point is that the satisfaction that goes along with involvement stems from one source, the exploratory drive, the need to get a better grip on reality, the intrinsic interest in how things and people are, the urge to experience and figure things out.

Involvement is similar to the concept of 'flow' in adults in states of optimal experience, developed by Mihalyi Csikszentmihalyi (2000). In a state of flow the experience becomes its own reward as the person becomes lost in the process, experiencing deep concentration and enjoyment, clarity about their goals and progress in what they are doing, no fear of failure, a feeling of control, and interest in the activity for its own sake. Flow has been associated with increased performance in work, education and sports. Flow is associated with a strong sense of autonomy, being more likely in people who feel they can control events and so can concentrate on internal drives rather than be concerned with the external demands of others. People with a strong flow motivation show a mastery orientation, associating learning with feelings of curiosity, interest, excitement, concentration, absorption, challenge, and the need to seek and master difficulties. Flow is connected with embracing challenge and enjoying the process, but is decreased when there is pressure to achieve and when there are external tangible rewards. Research has demonstrated that in adults flow motivation remains stable over time (Baumann and Scheffer 2010), so helping children to develop these dispositions could be expected to have far-reaching effects in the long term.

Well-being

Along with the scale describing involvement levels, Ferre Laevers' well-being scale works in tandem to support full understanding of children's learning. Using both scales together recognizes that emotional and physical well-being is a necessary precondition for learning. As Laevers (2005: 4) explains:

> we first have to explore the degree in which children do feel at ease, act spontaneously, show vitality and self-confidence. All this indicates that their emotional well-being is o.k. and that their physical needs, the need for tenderness and affection, the need for safety and clarity, the need for social recognition, the need to feel competent and the need for meaning in life and moral value are satisfied.

The adult role in children's involvement

The EYFS themes of 'enabling environments' and 'positive relationships' offer a useful framework for considering the role of the adult. An environment which supports emotional well-being will be first on the agenda in any consideration of good practice. Considering the needs of each child to build relationships with warm, consistent and responsive adults as well as with peers should be seen as a foundation for supporting children's involvement in their learning.

Children making their own choices is a key factor in children's levels of involvement, highlighting the importance of a learning environment which includes plenty of opportunity for children freely to initiate their own activities. In the autonomous opportunity to choose, plan and lead their own activity children are able to focus at the edge of their competence, finding their own challenges.

Although adults can and do plan activities with specific learning objectives geared to what they have observed of children's interests and current learning, they can never accurately fascinate and challenge all the children in a group. In self-selected activities, however, each individual child can focus on what is currently of most personal interest, and can explore and repeat investigations to satisfy deep curiosity and a need for mastery. Adults can support children's absorptions by noticing what is fascinating to a child and planning to introduce into the environment resources and opportunities that will further challenge the child to engage further and develop their understanding.

Along with choice and well-planned, stimulating resources, an enabling environment will offer uninterrupted periods of time and space which free children to follow their ideas and become deeply involved.

Child-initiated activity does not imply a lack of interaction with supportive adults. Children may be supported to focus and maintain attention in a number of ways, through contingent response based on observing the individual child. Adults may sometimes support children to focus their attention, for instance by offering non-directive stimulation. Researchers have found that babies who focus more successfully on their play have mothers who frequently stimulate their attention in a non-obtrusive way, helping draw their attention back from passing distractions and effectively teaching the child to focus their own attention (Carlton and Winsler 1998). At times when a child is clearly involved and concentrating, the sensitive adult might make the decision to guard the learning moment and avoid distracting the child's attention.

Practitioners who are aware that their stimulation and talk can be important supports for children's learning may sometimes feel an onus to interact almost constantly with children – but this can become interference rather than support. It is important for adults to observe carefully, ask themselves whether their interaction would be of use and in what way, and only then decide whether to become involved in the child's activity. One possibility is to become involved afterwards and talk with the child about their experience as a review rather than at the moment of concentration.

Where a child's interest is fleeting, renewed focus might be stimulated by playing alongside, modelling possibilities, introducing new elements or resources, refocusing through shared attention. A child who is over-stimulated and too excited to pay attention may be supported by offering a calmer environment or an island of calm in a one-to-one interaction.

As well as children experiencing the innate satisfaction from states of deep involvement and concentration, a further aim of effective adult support is for children gradually to become aware of and able to regulate their own learning – including knowing how important their concentration is. Children are very sensitive to what adults value, and adults can communicate the importance of committing energy and focus to activities by explicitly acknowledging when they have observed children showing deep curiosity and involvement. Children need to know that adults value the process of wondering, of losing yourself in something interesting which can grow increasingly complex, rather than looking for quick answers or showing interest in products only.

Keeping on trying

We learn from having a go at new things and giving the new experiences our full concentration. If we stay within the safe zone of what we already know how to do we are sure to be successful – but we don't learn anything new. It is only from meeting a challenge just beyond what we can currently do that we have the opportunity to develop new skills and understanding, and this carries a built-in risk that we won't be successful in our efforts. It may require several trial-and-error attempts, learning each time from what went wrong, before we achieve our goal. It may be that in unsuccessful attempts we didn't apply enough effort or concentration, or needed to stick with it longer.

Persisting in the face of difficulties is an essential ability for strong learners. The most successful people do not find that everything comes easily, but are familiar with trying hard and bouncing back from setbacks. This resilience is summed up in the familiar phrase, 'If at first you don't succeed, try, try again.'

Babies and young children are carried through early challenges by their power of perseverance, practising each stage of their emerging skills until they are successful. A baby balancing on unsteady legs, taking the first few tentative steps before toppling to the floor, doesn't give up and decide to rely on cruising along holding on to the furniture for the rest of her life.

Maintaining the ability to persevere when things don't go well is rooted in a strong sense of autonomy, competence and a growth mindset, and in emotional well-being:

- believing that trying again, trying harder or in a different way will make a difference (my decisions and actions make a difference);

- not being afraid of errors (I can learn from what doesn't work);
- not being afraid of difficulty (I can improve with effort, and difficulty doesn't mean that I'm no good at this).

The adult role in children keeping on trying

While babies persevere in repeating their efforts to drive their development and learning, differences in persistence appear very early. There may be some temperamental factors, but research has shown that adult interaction affects how persistent children are towards reaching their goals. One study illustrated the importance of both the quality of interaction within a relationship and the opportunities in the environment. Babies who were more persistent and focused on goals at 6 months were found to be more competent at 13 months – and these were the babies who experienced more stimulation and responsiveness from their mothers and had experiences of responsive toys (Yarrow et al. 1982).

Another study which looked at parenting styles and babies' persistence and competence at 12 and 20 months concluded that the mothers' attitudes and behaviour affected their babies' persistence at mastering their environment. Babies were more persistent when their mothers sensitively supported babies' autonomy in their activities, responding to their child's attempts rather than attempting to control them (Grolnick et al. 1984).

Educators and parents are often encouraged to ensure that children are successful in their efforts and never left to fail, based on the assumption that self-esteem will suffer if children do not always experience themselves as able. The relevance of self-esteem to learning is questionable in any case, as repeated studies have found either no link or even a negative association (Baumeister et al. 2003). Self-esteem – holding oneself in high regard which may not be rooted in the reality of one's attributes – is not the same thing as a sense of self-efficacy as described by Albert Bandura. Self-efficacy is a belief in one's abilities to reach a goal in a particular situation and is based on experience of what one can do, including one's ability to manage challenging tasks and situations.

There is a fine line between scaffolding children to work successfully within their zone of proximal development and over-supporting children so that they never face real difficulty. Children need opportunities to struggle, to find that things go wrong, and to learn that persistence often pays off. Very able children for whom everything comes easily in their early education often under-achieve when they hit later challenges, through never having had opportunities to develop emotional resilience and strategies for dealing with difficulty.

Guy Claxton (2006) cautions against too carefully scaffolding children's learning: 'Helping (children) learn better is not the same as helping them become better learners. Effective support can easily create dependency, unless the teacher is continually looking for opportunities to dismantle the scaffolding, and build students' disposition to do their own supporting.' Gunilla Dahlberg (2000: 19) quotes Eric Bronfenbrenner's comment which recognizes that careful scaffolding can limit children's possibilities: 'For upbringing to be successful, there needs to be at least one crazy uncle around who astonishes.' As well as offering un-dreamed-of possibility thinking to support children's creativity, the 'crazy uncle' will not carefully scaffold opportunities for children but is likely to take them beyond their comfort zone, providing valuable experience of the risks and thrills that attend working in uncharted territory.

Adults can be effective at supporting children's persistence when they

- ensure the learning environment offers challenge so that children can find their own challenges in play;
- introduce stimulation and manageable challenge;
- offer encouragement and sensitive support as they allow children to remain in conditions of uncertainty and difficulty when they grapple with challenges.

Adults could remind themselves to keep their own goal firmly in mind: not to ensure children do not make errors or face problems nor to solve the problems for the child, but to support children to know that they can learn from their errors and face problems with a belief in the power of their own efforts.

Enjoying achieving what they set out to do

Having become interested enough to expend effort and energy in deep involvement, and persevered even if things didn't go smoothly, active learners will continue to be drawn to learning experiences through receiving the satisfaction of reaching their own goals. This reflects the importance of intrinsic motivation where the experience brings its own reward.

The emotional component of intrinsic mastery motivation is strong. Alison Gopnik (Gopnik et al. 1999: 162) describes the 'distinctive joy' of babies and young children who have made sense of a puzzling situation, while Pen Green practitioners talk about toddlers showing 'chuffedness' at their achievements. This sense of internal satisfaction when children have met their own goals is quite different from what occurs when children achieve a goal set by adults, encouraged and rewarded through extrinsic motivators.

Linked to the questionable emphasis on promoting self-esteem, it is common for early years practitioners to encourage positive behaviours by providing children with liberal amounts of praise and other rewards such as stickers. There is a danger, however, that this approach could backfire and lower children's intrinsic motivation. Managing children's behaviour through positive rewards is rooted in an assumption that children are not motivated unless the motivation is provided from outside, and conveys a message to children that the goal is set and performance is judged by the adult – in other words, it harms the child's sense of autonomy to choose their own goals and to find satisfaction in the process of mastery. Studies have shown that the child then identifies less with the activity and becomes less motivated to participate. As Bandura (1994) explains, 'goals can be applied in ways that breed dislikes rather than nurture interests. Personal standards promote interest when they create challenges and serve as guides for aspirations. But if goals assigned by others impose constraints and performance burdens, the pursuit can become aversive.'

Children do, of course, value the positive response of others – which lays a responsibility on adults to respond wisely. Injudicious use of praise and reward can divert a child from a mastery orientation and intrinsic pleasure in the activity, and encourage turning instead towards a performance orientation and extrinsic motivation. So while praise and rewards may seem to gain a desired response from the child and bring good feelings in the short term, the longer term effects can be to reduce a child's internal sense of control, confidence in their own processes and judgements, and ultimate learning power.

The adult role in children enjoying what they set out to achieve

The use of tangible extrinsic rewards such as stickers or star charts should be a prime target for a re-think in early years practice, as their regular use has been shown to strongly reduce young children's intrinsic motivation. It is again important for adults to keep their own goal in mind: not to train children to perform when someone will reward them, but to support children to reward and strengthen the drive within themselves.

There may be a useful role for such external motivators if used only occasionally, for a short period, or for a specific purpose. In situations where adults may decide that external motivation has a place, there is a distinction to be made between rewards which are doled out in the gift of someone else and not directly linked to the activity itself, and consequences linked to a behaviour which can be used as reinforcers. For example, a child with additional needs who is reluctant to try to walk may be encouraged to take a few steps by the adult placing a sweet at intervals just out of the child's reach. Reaching the chocolate is an immediate reinforcer of what walking can do, and will encourage the child to step towards the next one. Here the child can see that walking itself can give power and have a benefit, which is preferable to the adult saying 'Take three steps and then I will give you a sweet'. The hope is that the child will learn that walking is a useful skill, and the reinforcers can be withdrawn as soon as possible.

Praise is often used as an external motivator, and there is no doubt that people value positive responses from others. But positive feedback includes showing genuine interest and engaging in the detail of what a child has done.

Carol Dweck (2006: 205) cautions,

> How do you use praise? Remember that praising children's intelligence or talent, tempting as it is, sends a fixed mindset message. It makes their confidence and motivation more fragile. Instead, try to focus on the processes they used, their strategies, effort, or choices. Practise working the process praise into your interactions with your children.

Praise that is an empty comment such as 'well done', 'good girl', 'that's lovely', or labelling children such as 'you're so clever', 'you're very good at that' decrease intrinsic motivation. On the other hand, where praise gives clear feedback about the child's process in the activity it has been shown to improve intrinsic motivation – it is making it clear that the child's own actions make the difference and so supports the child's autonomy. Praise should be specific, linked to the child's behaviour and pointing out aspects that are important in successful learning – how the learner is involved, concentrates, persists, uses different strategies, problem-solves, and has ideas. Feedback can also involve a specific discussion about the competence shown, not as a judgement of the adult but as an opportunity to consider the child's role as the active agent – what has been achieved, what can be learnt from problems, or how the child might approach it another time.

Travelling with a different view

Active learning describes the way strong learners engage with the people, things and events they encounter. In the context of warm social interactions with peers and adults, children are motivated by the enjoyment and sense of belonging together and experience their own autonomy while gradually beginning to identify with the values and goals of the group. Establishing an orientation to active learning in the early years is an important potential for early education, and as such straddles the dual nature of childhood as both being and becoming: though being an active learner is a foundation for a lifetime it is built in the rich here-and-now quality of how children experience their childhood. As described by British philosopher R.S. Peters (1965: 110), 'To be educated is not to have arrived at a destination; it is to travel with a different view. What is required is not feverish preparation for something that lies ahead, but to work with a precision, passion, and taste at worthwhile things that lie at hand.'

References

Ames, C. and Archer, J. (1988) Achievement goals in the classroom: students' learning strategies and motivation processes, *Journal of Educational Psychology*, 80: 260–7.

Bandura, A. (1994) Self-efficacy, in V.S. Ramachaudran (ed.) *Encylopedia of Human Behaviour*, Vol. 4, pp. 71–81.

Baumann, N. and Scheffer, D. (2010) Seeking flow in the achievement domain: the achievement flow motive behind flow experience, *Motivation and Emotion*, 34.

Baumeister, R., Campbell, J., Krueger, J. and Vohs, K. (2003) Does high self-esteem cause better performance, interpersonal success, happiness, or healthier lifestyles? *Psychological Science in the Public Interest*, 4(1): 1–44.

Bronson, M. (2000) *Self-regulation in Early Childhood: Nature and Nurture*. New York: The Guilford Press.

Carlton, M. and Winsler, A. (1998) Fostering intrinsic motivation in early childhood classrooms, *Early Childhood Education Journal*, 25(3): 162–3.

Claxton, G. (2006) Expanding the capacity to learn: a new end for education? Paper presented at the British Educational Research Association Annual Conference, 6 September.

Csikszentmihalyi, M. (2000) *Beyond Boredom and Anxiety: Experiencing Flow in Work and Play*. San Francisco, CA: Jossey-Bass.

Dahlberg, G. (2000) Early childhood pedagogy in a changing world: a practice-oriented research project troubling dominant discourses. *Policy, Practice and Politics, NZEI Te Riu Roa Early Childhood Millennium Conference Proceedings*, 19.

Darnon, C., Muller, D., Schrager, S. and Pannuzzo, N. (2006) Mastery and performance goals predict epistemic and relational conflict regulation, *Journal of Educational Psychology*, 98(4): 766–76.

Deci, E. and Ryan, R.M. (1985) *Intrinsic Motivation and Self-determination in Human Behavior*. New York: Plenum.

Deci, E. and Ryan, R. (2000) The 'what' and 'why' of goal pursuits: human needs and the self-determination of behavior, *Psychological Inquiry*, 11(4): 227–68.

Dweck, C. (2006) *Mindset*. New York: Random House.

Dweck, C. and Leggett, E. (1988) A social-cognitive approach to motivation and personality, *Psychological Review*, 95: 256–73.

Gopnik, A., Meltzoff, A. and Kuhl, P. (1999) *How Babies Think*. London: Phoenix.

Grolnick, W., Bridges, L. and Frodi, A. (1984) Maternal control style and the mastery motivation of one-year-olds, *Infant Mental Health Journal*, 5: 72–82.

Grolnick, W., Kurowski, C. and Gurland, S. (1999) Family processes and the development of children's self-regulation, *Educational Psychologist*, 34(1): 3–14.

Hall, D. (1995) Children: Hands on, brains off?, *The Independent*, 22 October.

Katz, L. (2000) Last class notes, in D. Rothenberg (ed.) *Proceedings of the Lilian Katz Symposium, November 5 2000*, Issues in Early Childhood Education.

Laevers, F. (1993) Deep level learning: an exemplary application on the area of physical knowledge, *European Early Childhood Research Journal*, 1(1): 53–68.

Laevers, F. (2005) *Deep-level-learning and the Experiential Approach in Early Childhood and Primary Education*. Leuven: Katholieke Universiteit Leuven Research Centre for Early Childhood and Primary Education.

Lai, E. (2011) *Motivation: A Literature Review*, Research Report. Harlow: Pearson.

Peters, R.S. (1965) Education as initiation, in R.D. Archambault (ed.) *Philosophical Analysis and Education*. New York: Humanities Press.

Ruedy, E. and Nirenberg, S. (1990) *Where do I Put the Decimal Point?: How to Conquer Math Anxiety and Increase your Facility with Numbers*. New York: Henry Holt and Company.

Ryan, R. and Stiller, J. (1991) The social contexts of internalization: parent and teacher influences on autonomy, motivation and learning, in P. Pintrich and M. Maehr (eds) *Advances in Motivation and Achievement: Vol. 7: Goals and Self-regulatory Processes*. Greenwich, CT: JAI Press.

Yarrow, L., Morgan, G., Jennings, K., Harmon, R. and Gaiter, J. (1982) Infants' persistence at tasks: relationships to cognitive functioning and early experience, *Infant Behaviour and Development*, 5(2–4): 131–41.

5 Creating and thinking critically

Di Chilvers

'You read in the books the fire alarm went off. Shouldn't it turn *on* if there is a fire?' (Ewan, nearly 5 years old)

'Is this the number 'b'? Have we done that yet because I found it in Robert's name and I know that's a 'c' because we talked about that and I saw it in Michael's name?' (Jake, 5 years old)

This chapter looks at the processes involved in children creating and thinking critically, processes which enable us to understand what we observe children doing and to use this understanding to support their ongoing ideas, interests and fascinations. It refers to children's ideas and questions such as those above and the theory underpinning the nature of their thinking and learning.

The following is an example of a group of children who are involved in creating and thinking critically.

The children have spotted a pile of branches and leaves that have been left after the trees had been pruned and they begin to pile them on top of a fence structure that the practitioner has provided as a *provocation* for their ideas. Many children busily work together to gather the branches and balance them over the fence structure to create a roof for the house. The practitioner helps them check for 'holes' and they find more leaves to block them up; 'We're making a very good den' they say and start to sing and repeat 'It's getting bigger, it's getting bigger.' The collaborative play continues all morning as children's ideas continue to flow. Emily says 'We need some steps', and goes to find some hollow blocks and sets about making her steps. 'Let's make a carpet', Ryan suggests and goes to gather the leaves, shred them and cover the space inside the den. Other children start to help. Katy has found a ruler and starts to measure the sticks and the fence and Sarah has a play saw, so she trims the overlapping branches. George decides that it isn't dark enough in the den as the light is coming in through the fence walls, so he fixes that by fetching all the plastic blocks and lines them up next to the fence, and then carefully begins to pile others on top of them to block out the light. The play continues with children returning to it throughout the day.

These everyday observations of young children's involvement in their play, their ideas and questions illustrate well their capacity to engage in thoughtful, imaginative and creative thinking. While the three EYFS characteristics of 'playing and exploring', 'active learning' and 'creating and thinking critically' may be viewed separately in the documentation, the reality for children (and adults) is that they are all intrinsically meshed together with connections running between them that are hard to separate out. With this in mind practitioners always need to remember that the tangle of young children's thinking, learning and development is there for a reason – it's how they think and learn best. What the three characteristics do is help us to 'untangle' what we have seen and observed in order to make sense of the complexities of children's learning and development, while always remembering that children's thinking needs to remain tangled in order for it to make sense to them. This is all about seeing young children's learning and development as a holistic process.

The characteristic of creating and thinking critically is 'untangled' further as it is broken down into the following aspects (Early Education 2012):

- **having their own ideas**, which involves children being curious and imaginative, prepared to 'have a go' at solving problems and to find new ways to do things;
- **making links** where children notice patterns in the ways things happen and in their experiences, make predictions about what may happen and test their ideas. Children develop ideas of grouping and categorizing, sequencing and cause and effect;
- **choosing ways to do things**, which includes children planning how to approach a task, solve a problem or reach a goal. They check how things are going and can change strategy if appropriate as well as review how well the approach worked.

All these aspects weave together as children play and explore and learn actively. By being authentic partners in thinking and learning, they have a central part to play in their own learning and development. In the observations at the beginning of this chapter we see children having their own ideas, making links and choosing ways to do things. There is much for the children to think about and puzzle over as well as reason and problem – solve as they grapple with the processes of thinking, understanding and learning. Observations like this are a window into the way children's minds are working and enable us to tune into their thought processes and emerging understanding of the complicated world they inhabit. Their thoughts and ideas are creative and unique to them, which, as Drummond et al. suggest, is a privilege to witness and be part of. 'When we work with children, when we play and talk with them, when we watch them and everything they do, we are witnessing a fascinating and inspiring process: we are seeing young children learn' (Drummond et al. 1993: 5). They go on to suggest that it is through these observations in everyday practice that we think about what we see, and 'strive to understand it and then put our understanding to good use' (p. 5).

The language of thinking

Before and after birth children's brains develop and their early experiences combine together to construct their thinking, understanding and knowledge. There is clear evidence now that children's early experiences – particularly those which are connected to attachment, nurturing and attunement – will shape their future engagement in learning (Elfer 2006; Trevarthen 1988 and 2006; Allen 2011; Whitebread 2012). Children's thinking and learning are often viewed and interpreted in isolation from their emotional and social well-being with little understanding of the connections in the brain and the fine networks that are forged through these early experiences. Disconnecting these naturally formed bonds through a compartmentalized view of children's learning, and focusing on what they learn rather than how they learn, creates a superficial and simple view of teaching, and runs the risk of disempowering children as thinkers and learners. Children's social and emotional development supports them in the process of thinking of ideas, solving problems, making links and choosing strategies in all sorts of complex, sophisticated and above all, connected ways. We saw examples in the children's questioning and play at the beginning of this chapter.

These processes can be described as the child's *language for thinking*, since constructing and then communicating thinking and creative ideas are a form of expression; they are ways of making thinking visible. Children who are pre-verbal or have no spoken language can all communicate their thinking through action. It is no coincidence that babies and toddlers have an innate drive and instinctual need to explore, play and follow their spontaneous, 'of the moment', urges. We can see this particularly in early schematic behaviours as children become fascinated with objects that roll, spin and pop up. We can also see it in the children's play (above) – as they build the den and follow their emerging ideas, they are sparked off by each other and supported by the practitioner. The combination of children creating and thinking critically and through their play is a potent association.

Creative and critical thinking as a process

The view of thinking and learning as a process is grounded in the theories of Bruner and Vygotsky as they made the case for children's thinking unfolding alongside their first-hand experiences, in a social context and as part of their mental architecture; with periods of challenge and struggle which, if supported, build and extend their thinking and learning in a meaningful way. Babies and young children are involved in this process right from the start as they instinctively explore the people, places and things within their immediate world, 'hoovering' up experiences which they then accumulate and add to previous ones. Many readers will be familiar with Reggio Emilia pedagogy where the message is clear, *all* children are competent and creative thinkers and learners. This belief forms the basis of their early years philosophy which includes the principle that children's development grows from their emergent and ongoing ideas as part of a process of constructing learning (Edwards et al. 1998; Rinaldi 2006).

In this process of construction, which is more effective when undertaken in collaboration with other children and adults, children's thinking is tried and tested with problems created and problems solved in a familiar and safe context of co-construction. If we watch this process we see the unique ways in which children are creatively making sense of their world in genuinely thoughtful ways, as Ewan and Jake are doing through their questions at the beginning of this chapter. It makes perfect sense that a fire alarm should be switched on if there is a fire, an idea which needs to be treated with value and respect since, 'Creativity is part of the process through which children begin to find out they have something unique to "say" in words, dance, music, or hatching out their theory' (Bruce 2004: 14).

The process of creative and critical thinking has been unravelled in various theories both historically, as with Bruner, Piaget and Vygotsky in the early twentieth century, and more recently in work undertaken by Robson (2006), Fumoto et al. (2012) and Craft (2012). Robson (2006: 172) builds on the ideas of Meadows (1993) and Claxton (1998) when she describes the creative process of thinking in four steps: *familiarization, incubation, insight* and *verification* (see Table 5.1). This is not a neat sequential process, travelling in tidy steps; it is a messy weaving together of ideas and experiences which, as they flow, create more complex thinking and understanding. This is the creative and critical thinking process, not just for young children but for all children; processes which will be used throughout life. However, while the four steps of familiarization, incubation, insight and verification offer us a framework for understanding children's creating and thinking critically there are other connected elements to consider.

The language of the imagination

Imagination is fundamental to children's creative and critical thinking; it is a significant part of the language of thinking which enables children to create and visualize their own ideas in unique and imaginative ways, as well as being able to engage in complex processes of thinking which involve memory, perception and abstract thinking. The children's imaginative 'den play' mentioned at the beginning of this

Table 5.1 Familiarization, incubation, insight and verification

	Explanation	In practice
Familiari-zation	Information gathering, acquiring expertise, testing out ideas. Becoming familiar with people, places and things and finding out about the immediate world around you. Collaborating and playing with others as a social, communicative process	We can clearly see these actions and thoughts as children play and experiment. Babies sensory exploration of objects as they put everything into their mouths; toddlers repetitive actions, curiosity and beginning to question by pointing and asking why; older children puzzling out and problem solving to find out how to make things work and recreate their ideas. In the 'den-making' example children are familiarizing themselves with the materials and shaping their ideas as they play – one child's idea sparks off another's.
Incubation	A period of absorption, reflection and thinking; taking time to process the idea or information and make sense of it in order to make it your own. Time to generate even more ideas, develop your own perspective and have an opportunity to think about your thinking. This can often be a solitary process where children digest what they have experienced. Bruce (2004) refers to this as incubating and hatching your ideas with an important period of 'simmering'.	Babies, toddlers and young children all need the time and space to think, play and repeat. It is important to make sure that they have the time and space to do this both on their own and with others. Observation of children's facial expressions, body posture and complete involvement as they ponder and mull over their actions and thinking will give us the clues to their creativity, as long as we are observing them while they are engrossed in their own activities. Jake and Ewan have clearly incubated and simmered their ideas, digesting the information they already have, thinking about and trying to make sense of it by asking thoughtful questions.
Insight	A connection is made and children reach that moment of 'illumination' or 'insight'. This could happen in a flash or may be more of a gentle unfolding of understanding; in either case the child's thinking has deepened.	Observation of child-led play and activities (including babies and toddlers) shows us the moment when something has happened, e.g. Jake has made the connection between letters and sounds and how they form words – he has mastered the abstractness of symbols and understood that they have meaning. With babies and toddlers, insight often comes with actions, e.g. knowing that the doll hasn't completely disappeared when mummy hides it behind her back.
Verification	Children check out their thinking and re-test it in other contexts in order to establish and refine their understanding	Children (including babies and toddlers) use play to verify their thinking and understanding. If we observe how children are interpreting their thinking through their play we can verify our understanding (and judgements) as to their progress. For example George has identified a problem with the den (it's not dark enough) so he uses his previously acquired experiences to solve the problem – he sets about refining his knowledge of light and dark through his play. We can gather from this that he has understood the difference between the two and how to recreate darkness.

chapter gives an insight into these complex processes. By deconstructing what is happening we can gain a better understanding of why being able to play in an imaginative way is essential 'brain exercise' for becoming a creative and critical thinker.

The 'den play' has been provoked by the responsive practitioner who made sure that the branches from the tree pruning were left in a pile for the following day. The practitioner knew how important it was to provide such a provocation for children to have their own ideas. This open-ended, imaginative material was enough to spark ideas and generate children's imagination; they had a vision or an idea of what they wanted to do which was individual at first and then became collaborative. Duffy (1998) explains this process as children visualizing and creating exciting possibilities from the ideas they have in order to make meaning of their thinking; a creative process which is essential to creators of IT software, innovative design and engineering. If there are no limits on children's imagination and their creative possibilities then their thinking can flow as they familiarize and incubate the experience.

Csikszentmihalyi (1996) has written at length about the 'state of flow' in humans' ability to become so engrossed in what they are doing that they become unaware of time, cannot be distracted and are fully focused on the task in hand. This is the same for children, where they become deeply involved in something, usually that they have initiated, and they become lost in it, concentrating for long periods and persisting even when the going gets tough. It is at moments like this that children's thinking and learning move into another dimension and become more meaningful, eventually leading to higher levels of 'mastery' and understanding. Laevers (2005) has also made the connection between children's involvement in their play/activities and their flow of concentration, persistence and energy, which he describes as 'intense mental activity' leading to deeper levels of thinking and learning. We have already mentioned the importance of play and exploration for creating and thinking critically and here we see an overlap with active learning. (See Chapter 4 for more on the importance of involvement and persistence.)

It is through imaginative play that children make meaning of their (and others') ideas and are able to think things through as they simmer or incubate their thinking and refine and extend what they know. Claxton (2000) refers to children having a 'learning toolkit' which expands throughout life and contains the critical components of being a confident and capable 'learner'. He includes imagination in the tool kit for the following reasons:

> Learning by imagination is the ability to extend what we know and can do by creating imaginary worlds. You can play and push things to the limit and test your understanding to destruction. You can weave new patterns inside your mind from the different bits of information that you've picked up from the world around you.
>
> (Claxton 2000: 6)

The combination of the flow of thinking, deep involvement and imagination all contribute to the child's repertoire of learning, deepening their understanding and moving their learning into much more sophisticated zones of thinking, particularly sustained shared thinking. At this point in their imaginative play children will be exploring and sharing their ideas with others, trying to solve problems and develop their thinking together – constructing their own thinking and learning. For example as Emily decides to add the steps, Ryan suggests the den needs a carpet, and George is on a mission to make it darker; they have all added their imaginative ideas to the 'project'; they have collectively moved their thinking on, giving reasons for their decisions and working out how to fulfil them. Siraj-Blatchford et al. (2002) explain this process as 'when an adult and a child or two children work together in an intellectual way to solve a problem, clarify a concept, evaluate activities or extend a narrative' (p. 8).

The REPEY project (Siraj-Blatchford et al. 2002: 12) gave clear evidence that child-initiated play alongside 'teacher initiated group work' were the 'main vehicles for learning', especially if they were embedded in play that had been started by the child/children. Other research (Siraj-Blatchford 2008; Whitebread 2012) has shown us that young children become more involved and engrossed in learning if they are encouraged and allowed to follow their interests, either as a group or individually. When this happens they will concentrate for much longer periods, persist at challenges and look for ways to do things by using reasoning and problem-solving skills.

Whitebread (2012) (see also Chapter 2) has identified the key elements for self-regulation in early years pedagogy and they can be associated with children's creating and thinking critically. They include the following;

- initiation of activities by children – whereby they make the decisions about what to play, where and who with; setting their own meaningful goals and challenges;
- opportunities to play and work by themselves without adult direction; self-directed learning and self-resolution of problems;
- extensive collaboration and talk; making thinking and learning visible through communication and language.

These elements are all inherent in the development of children's cognitive self-regulation where they are taking responsibility for their own learning, are intrinsically self-motivated to engage in the challenge of thinking and learning and become actively involved in the process. The 'den play' was completely driven by the children, apart from the adult's initial provocation of the branches, and lasted most of the day with children returning to their imaginative play. The adult intervened from time to time as she saw that children needed help or support and occasionally added a further provocation which extended the thinking further.

Imaginative play – moving from concrete to symbolic thinking

The language of imaginative thinking takes children from their current, in the moment, concrete experiences, to those which are much more sophisticated and abstract; the roots of this being in children's play: 'the projection into an imaginary world stretches their conceptual abilities and involves a development in their abstract thought. The complexity involved in this process makes imagination the highest level of early development (Vygotsky 1978)' (Duffy 1998: 53).

The complexity begins early on as children represent their ideas through play, for example an older baby plays hidey-boo and claps to show enjoyment, repeating the game by covering their eyes, or a toddler begins to feed the dolly and rock it to sleep (see Chapter 3 for more detail on this process). For older children the play becomes more complex and imaginative as materials are given meaning. For example the box is a roller coaster, a piece of fabric becomes an invisible cloak and the red water is a potion. Children become increasingly creative in the ways that they attach meaning to objects, as long as the objects leave room for the imagination. The messages they are learning are about the way in which meaning can be attached to all kinds of things. In terms of their creating and critical thinking, they begin to notice patterns and sequences and cause and effect. Ewan and Jake are beginning to understand this in their thoughtful questioning of the things which puzzle them; they are seeking clarification/verification of their thinking.

Children then have to make the connection between their own symbols and those which are created by the culture and systems around them. For example cultures imbue meaning into symbols which represent sounds, letters and words, so the word 'house' is agreed to mean a place you might live, though it becomes more complicated when they are also called 'bungalows', 'terraces' and 'flats', etc. but generally everyone understands what these words mean. There is also the symbolic language of mathematics, music and the modern abstractness of text messaging. Children have to make sense of the meaning and not just the word and they have to learn how to read and write using the agreed symbols. The more opportunities children have to think flexibly and play imaginatively in this representational way the more likely they can make the leap from concrete to symbolic forms of thinking.

Children have a complex system of symbols with which to become familiar yet they eagerly embrace the challenges involved by being curious, motivated and connected to wanting to make sense of it all. Playing imaginatively is one of the most important opportunities we can provide to help them in this quest, however imaginative play is often marginalized and seen as a frivolous activity which you can engage in when all the 'real work' is done. As the play versus work argument continues, even when there is clear evidence to support its value, children are channelled early into the formal aspects of literacy and numeracy at the very time when they need to be following the pathways of familiarization, incubation, insight and verification. Some questions to reflect on are:

- What status does imaginative play have in your setting or school?
- What opportunities are there for all the children to engage in imaginative play both indoors and outdoors?
- Whose imagination are you following – the children's or your own? Who decides?
- How much time are children given to think about and incubate their imaginative ideas?
- Are the materials you offer open-ended?
- Are children using imaginative language and asking imaginative and creative questions like Ewan and Jake?
- How often are children able to reflect upon and revisit their thinking?

The language of reflection – being creative and critical

Creative thinking could be described as the zone in which children's ideas and thoughts blossom and emerge in unique and genuine ways, especially through rich and varied imaginative play; while critical thinking is more aligned to the processes that support creative thinking.

Being reflective and thinking about our thinking (known as metacognition) is on the edge of both these views; on the one hand reflection is part of being creative as ideas blossom through collaboration and joint thinking while, on the other hand, it is part of a metacognitive process which supports the development of critical thinking. Either way, opportunities to reflect and think in a metacognitive way are a central part of children being and becoming competent and capable thinkers and learners.

Reflection-in-action (Schön 1987) was evident as the children played together in creating the den and individual ideas sparked off other ideas as they talked about what they were doing and why. At lunchtime the practitioner shared with the children some of the photographs and dialogue she had documented during the morning which all led to further discussion, reflection and thinking (reflection-on-action). In the afternoon the children returned to the den play and carried on with the 'jobs' they had identified. Creative and critical thinking had moved forward in this constructive process; the children had authentic ownership of their thinking and learning which made it a meaningful experience. A very important part of this process was making links and noticing patterns in their experience, making predictions, testing their ideas and changing strategy as needed.

Metacognition can be explained as 'thinking about thinking' (Robson 2006: 82), 'knowing what to do when you don't know what to do' (Claxton 1999) and 'spontaneous wonderings' (Donaldson 1978). It is how children become aware of themselves as thinkers and how they reflect on their thinking, but in order to do this they have to have their thinking and ideas recognized and acknowledged by the people around them.

Siraj-Blatchford (2008) has shown that this process is at the heart of children's learning and contributes significantly to their belief in themselves as learners and the thinking dispositions they need for learning to learn. The practitioner who provoked the den play supported this, in practice, by being aware of children's thinking and letting them talk about their ideas/thoughts together, giving them the time to wonder, ponder, think and reflect; enabling the children to become involved in defining the problem and looking for solutions and working together, collaboratively as a 'community of learners.'

Reflection is an integral part of pedagogy in Reggio Emilia philosophy where children constantly share and discuss their ideas and thinking in collaborative partnerships; metacognitive discussions are a regular part of the day and emerge out of the children's current ideas. The following is a conversation between a group of children (all aged 5) in a Reggio Emilia pre-school. They are talking about the city and how it is connected (Giudici and Rinaldi 2001: 239)

Giacomo:	In the squares there are people talking
Simone:	There are pretty squares and ugly ones. Then there are some squares for parked cars and for soccer players
Giacomo:	I think they don't work well because the people don't know where to be
Simone:	Cities are all connected by the streets and the railroads, right. Giacomo?
Giacomo:	Well, yeah, the streets are important for keeping the city together and for making it work
Emiliano:	We need to see if it's all connected
Simone:	Like in real cities
Giacomo:	We need to make sure that the whole city is connected and that nobody gets lost.

The boys' discussion and co-construction makes them think about some complex social and strategic issues – how to make the roads work! They are busy talking, reflecting and symbolizing their ideas in drawing and mapping out the roads, the piazzas and the city of Reggio Emilia. They bounce ideas backwards and forwards and even ask each other questions to verify their thinking. These metacognitive discussions begin early on in the Reggio pre-schools and are probably one of the main reasons why the children, in the main, are such creative and critical thinkers as they are supported to follow their own ideas and their flow of thought.

In Reggio pedagogy, reflective practice and metacognitive thinking are also supported through the process of documentation, where children's unfolding ideas and hypotheses are captured through a process of observation, documenting the flow of children's play/activities as a narrative, interpreting what has been observed by making informed judgements and keeping children's thinking, interests, ideas and talk central. The documentation weaves together teaching, learning, assessment and planning in order to make the process of thinking and understanding relevant and meaningful to the children as Rinaldi (in Giudici and Rinaldi 2001: 84) explains:

> Observation, documentation and interpretation are woven together into what I would define as a 'spiral movement', in which none of these actions can be separated out from the others. It is impossible, in fact, to document without observing and interpreting. By means of documenting, the thinking – or the interpretation – of the documenter becomes tangible and capable of being interpreted.

In practice the process of documentation is undertaken with the children; for example as the children continued to explore their city of Reggio, the practitioners were recording the conversations they had, taking sequences of photographs to document the narrative of the children's thinking as it evolved, photocopying drawings and maps in stages as the children kept coming back to add more and refine them and generally gathering together evidence of the children's ideas and thinking. This was then brought together by the practitioners to reflect upon and decide ways in which to support and extend the thinking. It is then re-presented to the children and referred to as they take their learning forwards. The children reflect back on previous experiences, discuss them and move onto other ideas in a cycle of metacognitive thinking. This review process is also central to the HighScope approach (Holt 2010) and illustrates very well how practitioners can effectively support the processes involved in the EYFS strand of creating and thinking critically – 'choosing ways to do things':

- Planning, making decisions about how to approach a task, solve a problem and reach a goal
- Checking how well their activities are going
- Changing strategy as needed
- Reviewing how well the approach worked

(Early Education 2012: 8)

The positive relationship and enabling environment columns in *Development Matters* (Early Education 2012) also provide some practical examples of how adults could support children's thinking through the language they use.

The language of possibility thinking

Craft (2010: 20) describes possibility thinking as 'allowing us to transform *what is* to *what might be'* (original emphasis) in order to develop ideas and thinking through a process of questioning, self-expression, imagining, collaborative view sharing and taking risks. For example Jake's possibility question about the letters shows some confusion with number symbols, which is clarified as his question goes on; from what we can tell he does have a good understanding of the symbolic structure of letters and sounds. This is an inherent part of possibility thinking which also includes 'a willingness and capacity to be immersed, to pose and respond to questions, to make connections, to use imagination, to innovate and to take risks' (Craft 2010: 20).

The seven points shown in Table 5.2 have been identified by Craft (Craft et al. 2007; Craft 2012) as being the key features of possibility thinking; they all connect to the examples of children's creating and thinking critically at the beginning of this chapter. Craft's research has shown that where children were able to weave in and out of these features in their play and early experiences their creativity and critical thinking moved to deeper levels of involvement and learning, particularly in being able to communicate and generate more ideas, talk and discuss them with others, become self-motivated and self-determined, engage in collaborative thinking and learning and take their ideas forward into unknown territory. Children had a sense of agency and control over their learning which supported their belief and confidence in themselves as creative and critical thinkers (Craft et al. 2007; Craft 2012).

The language of conversation to support the co-construction of thinking

The children in the examples at the beginning of the chapter are clearly able to communicate and express their thinking, ideas and interests. The articulation of their thinking comes through their inquisitive questions and the conversations the children have as they play together. While spoken language isn't the only way to communicate your thinking (remember The One Hundred Languages – Edwards et al. 1998) it is certainly one of the best ways to share what is happening in your head in a social and reflective way. Talking clarifies thinking and can lead to the generation of even more ideas, which in itself is creative and the kind of lifelong learning skill that all children need to have in the present and the future.

Conversational talk is particularly influential in constructing creative and critical thinking because of its informality and context in everyday experiences which are rich in opportunities. Importantly the conversations which *children start* are usually the ones that will develop into powerful and creative learning experiences. They mainly originate when children are involved in play, cannot be predicted or planned for, but provide a good foundation for learning which can be extended

Table 5.2 Seven key features of possibility thinking

Feature	How does this connect to the examples?
Question posing and question responding – finding the perfect possibility question which is neither too narrow (closed) nor too broad (too general), both of which would affect children's creative and critical thinking. Questions have different roles: Leading questions will drive the children's activity – with more control from the question asker (child or adult) Service questions enable children to develop strategies to help them undertake the leading question Follow-through questions are the finer questions which help to fulfil an idea	In the 'den play' children's questions were leading, e.g. 'Let's make a carpet!' and 'We need some steps?' They posed the possibilities and then set about making them happen A service question would be 'How can I find enough leaves to cover all of it?' A follow-through question would be 'Do I need to find big leaves to cover it all up?'
Play – which is open-ended, creative and imaginative with adults who participate and become involved as play partners, 'offering possibilities in terms of where children might take their play' (Craft 2012: 57). Play with high cognitive challenge – as described in the children's imaginative play. Providing props, continuous provision, plenty of time and space	The 'den play' was full of possibilities which the practitioner left the children to decide upon – she observed what they were doing and saying, participated playfully from time to time and provided further props such as a tarpaulin Children were able to move in and out of the play throughout the day and the rest of the week
Immersion – or incubation. Time to become lost in the play and involved in a safe and secure enabling environment with practitioners who respect, support and value children's ideas and thinking	The children's ideas for the den were followed by the adults who enjoyed being outside with them and sharing in the excitement of the collaborative project. Any pre-defined planning was dropped in order to follow the flow of thinking
Innovation – or insight. Children make connections between their ideas which support the development of their understanding and take their thinking forward	Ewan and Jake's thoughtful questions show how they are connecting their own ideas in creative ways and taking their thinking forward
Being imaginative. See above – children need to engage in imagining what might be – the possibilities. Taking ownership of their ideas and translating them through their play	Very evident in the 'den play' where children were making careful decisions about what needed doing and how to do it. Their imaginative experiences of constructing the den brought together a wide range of skills, attitudes and dispositions
Self-determination and risk taking. Children become deeply involved and self-motivated with adults encouraging children to try things out and 'have a go' in a safe, and supportive enabling environment	The enabling environment of the nursery garden, with open-ended possibilities and huge branches off the pollarded trees gave an element of risk in a secure, supportive and creative setting. Practitioners encouraged children's own decision making and self-regulation

Source: Adapted from Craft et al. (2007) and Craft (2012).

by the children or a sensitive practitioner who has observed, listened and then participated (Siraj-Blatchford et al. 2002). It is the 'serve and return' (Harvard University Centre on the Developing Child 2012) model of co-construction which Loris Malaguzzi (Edwards et al. 1998) describes as a game of 'ping pong' (table tennis) and is created when the conversation flows from one aspect to another, with the participants batting ideas, possibility questions and thinking to each other in such a way that no one misses the ball! As a result creative thinking is co-constructed in a situation of 'joint involvement' or sustained shared thinking.

The following points, adapted from Chilvers 2006, highlight some of the finer detail of creative, conversational language where children can . . .

- **formulate ideas:** talking generates ideas and thinking at any age. A baby will babble with delight as she controls a game of 'I drop the rattle and you pick it up' and a 3-year-old will chatter as he tries to work out how to make the wheels turn on the car he has just made. Sensitive support from an adult and repetition of single words will help this babble and chatter become words and logical thought.
- **confirm and clarify what they think:** by talking about experiences, including learning, young children can reaffirm themselves and gain confidence in what they are doing. They can check and re-check their ideas collaboratively.
- **reflect:** speaking involves reflection – thinking, for example, about past experiences or what they have just done and engaging in conversation. 'I remember when . . .' or 'When I was a baby did I . . .?', 'The last time I did this it . . .'
- **make their ideas and thinking visible:** in a conversation the child's ideas and thinking are made visible and are usually related to something which is of interest to them and based in the reality and context of their lives, e.g. 'Why does the snow disappear?' Or 'Why can't I jump as high as the cat?' It is only by giving children endless opportunities to talk that we can begin to understand what is going on in their heads. We also need to pay attention to where they are going next in order to support their developing language and thought – often by modelling the process ourselves.
- **build their confidence and self-esteem:** confidence and self-esteem arise out of being listened to and accepted. One of the key ways in which this happens is through children's conversation. If children's own conversations are accepted they quickly learn that their views, ideas and talk are valued. Through conversation children gain affirmation and the courage to contribute as well as being able to express their own needs, wishes and thoughts. They will become more in touch with themselves and develop a sense of positive well-being.

Observing the language of thinking

If we are expecting that children become more reflective and engage in metacognition as part of the development of their creative and critical thinking then it seems only fair that the people who work with them also pursue this goal. Observing children's thinking, ideas and interests unfold is one of the most effective ways to do this as practitioners are involved in the reflective observation cycle seen in Figure 5.1 (Early Education 2012). This cycle is explored in more detail by Judith Stevens in Chapter 6.

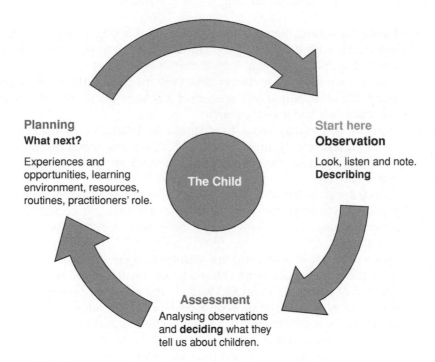

Figure 5.1 The Observation, Assessment and Planning Cycle.
Source: Early Education (2012). (Reproduced under the terms of the Open Government Licence.)

Observation is the practitioner's opportunity to watch children's creative and critical thinking unfold, which usually happens in moments which are spontaneous, unplanned and start from the child/children. If we really want to understand how the child is thinking and what they know we just have to watch them and document it in some way.

Integral to achieving this, it seems to us, is reflective practice, in which *teachers stand back,* to consider what children are telling them though their engagement in the classroom. It also involves *documenting these moments in some way*, as a mental snapshot, as actual still or moving images, as notes, or in special circumstances as recordings which may be later played back. Documentation enables us to note and respond to pertinent events, responses and comments.

(Craft et al. 2007: 9, original emphasis)

It is important to remember that it is the process or narrative of the child/children's creating and thinking critically thinking which needs to be observed and recorded. Taking single snapshots at the beginning and/or end will not illustrate the whole picture; it is the 'bit in the middle' that tells the story of the thinking and provides those incredible moments when you have witnessed children reaching a point of understanding and real mastery.

Assessment is the way that we make sense of what we have seen; Craft et al. (2007: 9) call this 'reflecting on what we learn from both standing back and

As you observe children in their play, indoors and outdoors, did you see children using the language of thinking? Note down what you saw, take sequenced photographs or film and use this to make an informed judgement about children's progress. Think about the following and discuss it together with others in your setting or school.		
Aspects/processes	**What does this mean?**	**Did you see this happening as you observed the children? What did it look like?**
Familiarization		
Incubation		
Insight		
Verification		
Imaginative play		
Imaginative play – moving from concrete to symbolic thinking		
Reflection Metacognition		
Possibility thinking		
Conversational language and co-construction		

Figure 5.2 Observing the language of thinking.

documenting, in order to appropriately support and stimulate their learning'. At this point we are trying to unpick the holistic nature of children's thinking, development and learning; looking for the language of thinking as well as the 'tools' children use for thinking, such as problem setting and problem solving, hypothesizing and reasoning, asking questions and possibility thinking. It is only then that we can make an informed, professional judgement about children's progress, especially about *how* they are learning (the characteristics of learning) as well as what they are learning (the seven areas of learning, DfE 2012). Figure 5.2 may be helpful in clarifying your own thinking and understanding of these critical aspects of young children's development.

Planning is the way in which children's development is supported and taken forward and should be a collaborative partnership approach between the adult leading the way and planning play, activities and focused groups and children initiating ideas and being creative. If this doesn't happen and the adult is planning and structuring every minute of the day there will be few, if any, opportunities for children to undertake their own journeys in creative and critical thinking.

Final thoughts

The language of children's thinking is the foundation of children's creative and critical thinking, on which they can grow in confidence, self-assurance and well-being with a real belief in themselves as competent and capable thinkers and learners. They are also the lifelong learning attitudes, skills and dispositions we would want people to have for the future. 'In the early 21st century we recognise that being creative is one of the defining characteristics of all human beings' (Craft 2010: 2).

References

Allen, G. (2011) *Early Intervention: The Next Steps*. London: HM Government.

Bruce, T. (2004) *Cultivating Creativity in Babies, Toddlers and Young Children*. London: Hodder and Stoughton.

Chilvers, D. (2006) *Young Children Talking: The Art of Conversation and Why Children Need to Chatter*. London: Early Education.

Claxton, G. (1998) *Hare Brain, Tortoise Mind*. London: Fourth Estate.

Claxton, G. (1999) *Wise Up: Learning to Live the Learning Life*. Stafford: Network Educational Press Ltd.

Claxton, G. (2000) A sure start for an uncertain world. Transcript of a lecture, *Early Education Journal*, Spring 2000. London: Early Education.

Craft, A. (2010) Teaching for possibility thinking – what is it and how do we do it? *Learning Matters*, 15(1): 19–23.

Craft, A. (2012) Child-initiated play and professional creativity: enabling four-year-olds' possibility thinking, *Thinking Skills and Creativity Journal*, 7: 48–61.

Craft, A., Cremin, T., Burnard, P. and Chappell, K. (2007) Developing creative learning through possibility thinking with children aged 3–7, in A. Craft, T. Cremin and P. Burnard (eds) *Creative Learning 3–11 and How We Document it*. London: Trentham Books.

Csikszentmihalyi, M. (1996) *Creativity*. New York: HarperCollins.

DCSF (Department for Children, Schools and Families) (2008) *Statutory Framework for the Early Years Foundation Stage: Setting the Standards for Learning, Development and Care for Children from Birth to Five*. Nottingham: DCSF Publications.

DfE (Department for Education) (2012) *Statutory Framework for the Early Years Foundation Stage: Setting the Standards for Learning, Development and Care for Children from Birth to Five*. http://www.foundationyears.org.uk/early-years-foundation-stage-2012/ or http://www.education.gov.uk/aboutdfe/statutory/g00213120/eyfs-statutory-framework (accessed 1 January 2013).

Donaldson, M. (1978) *Children's Minds*. London: Fontana Press.

Drummond, M.J., Rouse, D. and Pugh, G. (1993) *Making Assessment Work: Values and Principles in Assessing Young Children's Learning*. London: NES Arnold/National Children's Bureau.

Duffy, B. (1998) *Supporting Creativity and Imagination in the Early Years*. Buckingham: Open University Press.

Early Education (2012) *Development Matters in the Early Years Foundation Stage*. London: Early Education. Available from www.early-education.org.uk and for download at http://www.foundationyears.org.uk/early-years-foundation-stage-2012/ (accessed 20 December 2012).

Edwards, C., Gandini, L. and Forman, G. (1998) *The Hundred Languages of Children, The Reggio Emilia Approach – Advanced Reflections*, 2nd edn. Westport, CT: Ablex Publishing.

Elfer, P. (2006) Exploring children's expressions of attachment in nursery, *European Early Childhood Education Research Journal*, 14(2): 81–96.

Fumoto, H., Robson,S., Greenfield, S. and Hargreaves, D. (2012) *Young Children's Creative Thinking*. London: Sage.

Giudici, C. and Rinaldi, C. (eds) (2001) *Project Zero, Making Learning Visible – Children as Individual and Group Learners*. Reggio Emilia: Reggio Children srl.

Holt, V. (2010) *Bringing the High Scope Approach to your Early Years Practice*, 2nd edn. London: Routledge.

Harvard University Center on the Developing Child (2012) Serve and return interaction shapes brain circuitry. National Scientific Council on the Developing Child. www.developingchild.harvard.edu (accessed December 2012).

Laevers, F. (2005) *Deep-level-learning and the Experiential Approach in Early Childhood and Primary Education*. Leuven: Katholieke Universiteit.

Meadows, S. (1993) *The Child as Thinker*. London: Routledge.

Rinaldi, C. (2006) *In Dialogue with Reggio Emilia: Listening, Researching and Learning*. London: Routledge.

Robson, S. (2006) *Developing Thinking and Understanding in Young Children*. London: Routledge.

Schön, D. (1987) *Educating the Reflective Practitioner: Toward a New Design for Teaching and Learning in the Professions*. San Francisco, CA: Jossey-Bass Publishers.

Siraj-Blatchford, I., Sylva, K., Muttock, S., Gilden, R. and Bell, D. (2002) *Researching Effective Pedagogy in the Early Years (REPEY)*, DfES Research Report RR356. London: DfES.

Siraj-Blatchford, I. (2008) Understanding the relationship between curriculum, pedagogy and progression in learning in early childhood, *Hong Kong Journal of Early Childhood*, 7(2): 3–13.

Trevarthen, C. (1988). Universal co-operative motives: how infants begin to know the language and culture of their parents, in G. Jahoda and M. Lewis (eds) *Acquiring Culture: Cross Cultural Studies in Child Development*. Beckenham: Croom-Helm.

Trevarthen, C. (2006) 'Doing' education – to know what others know, *Early Education Journal Summer* 49, London: Early Education.

Vygtosky, L. (1978) *Mind in Society: The Development of Higher Psychological Processes*. Cambridge, MA: Harvard University Press.

Whitebread, D. (2012) *Developmental Psychology and Early Childhood Education*. London: Sage.

6 Observing, assessing and planning for how young children are learning

Judith Stevens

This chapter explores the observation, assessment and planning cycle and how it can support and extend children's learning. There are opportunities to reflect on the principles which underpin effective formative and summative assessment.

The chapter focuses on the inclusion of the 'characteristics of effective learning' in assessment and the shift from only *what* children learn to *how* they learn – a new component in the EYFS Profile. The EYFS Statutory Framework (DfE 2012b) requires early years practitioners to review children's progress and share a summary with parents at two points: in the prime areas between the ages of 24 and 36 months (the Progress Check at Age Two), and at the end of the EYFS (the EYFS Profile). The implications of this renewed emphasis on engaging parents in the assessment process are addressed. Overall, the chapter explores the need for flexibility in planning and keeping children at the heart of planning through tuning into young children's current enthusiasms and fascinations.

Since the introduction of the revised EYFS in September 2012, the renewed emphasis on *how* children learn as well as *what* they learn has puzzled some practitioners. The workforce appears to be divided into two schools of thought – those who are wondering what all the fuss is about, as they have always reflected on *how* children are learning, and those who really still aren't sure what this change in emphasis means for them.

The Statutory Framework for the EYFS paragraph 1.10 states:

> In planning and guiding children's activities, practitioners *must* reflect on the different ways that children learn and reflect these in their practice. Three characteristics of effective teaching and learning are:
>
> • playing and exploring – children investigate and experience things, and 'have a go'
> • active learning – children concentrate and keep on trying if they encounter difficulties, and enjoy achievements

- creating and thinking critically – children have and develop their own ideas, make links between ideas, and develop strategies for doing things.

Starting at the very beginning is generally a very good place to start, and it is important to get some idea of the 'big picture' of observation, assessment and planning and the principles which underpin the process.

The diagram on page 3 of *Development Matters* (Early Education 2012; reproduced as Figure 6.1 below) gives a clear overview of the observation, assessment and planning process, starting with, and *keeping* the child at the heart. Observation is the starting point for all assessment and planning.

Observing: describing what is happening

Assessing: analysing observations and deciding what they tell us about children

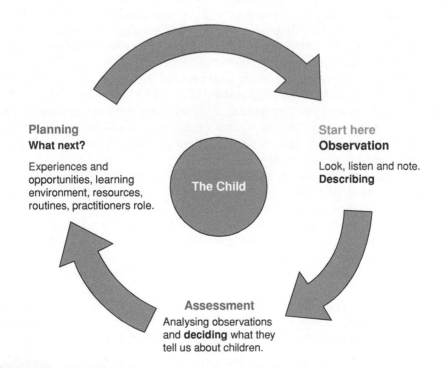

Planning
What next?

Experiences and
opportunities, learning
environment, resources,
routines, practitioners role.

The Child

Start here
Observation

Look, listen and note.
Describing

Assessment
Analysing observations
and **deciding** what they
tell us about children.

Figure 6.1 The Observation, Assessment and Planning Cycle.
Source: Early Education (2012). (Reproduced under the terms of the Open Government Licence.)

Planning: what next? Using observations and assessments to inform: experiences and opportunities; the indoor and outdoor learning environments; routines; resources and the role of the practitioner.

As we consider how the characteristics of effective learning fit within this observation, assessment and planning process, it is worth reflecting on how the process can be interpreted for both formative and summative assessment.

- **Formative assessment,** or assessment for learning – where assessment is part of, and supports learning and teaching
- **Summative assessment** – the periodic summary of formative assessments, which makes statements about children's achievements

The cycle is often thought of in terms of written observations and assessments used to inform planning for the next day or the next week. But, as was identified in *Learning, Playing and Interacting: Good Practice in the Early Years Foundation Stage* (DCSF 2009: 23) we need to think about how the process works on an ongoing, daily basis:

> Babies and young children, however, are experiencing and learning in the here and now, not storing up their questions until tomorrow or next week. It is in that moment of curiosity, puzzlement, effort or interest – the 'teachable moment' – that the skilful adult makes a difference. By using this cycle on a moment-by-moment basis, the adult will be always alert to individual children (observation), always thinking about what it tells us about the child's thinking (assessment), and always ready to respond by using appropriate strategies at the right moment to support children's well-being and learning (planning for the next moment).

Principles underpinning effective observation, assessment and planning

So, the very first thing we need to do is to keep the child at the heart of the observation, assessment and planning process. We need to observe children, analyse our observations in order to plan to build on what they know and can do, and support the ways in which they are learning. The second thing we need to remember is that observation, assessment and planning should not generate mountains of paperwork. Third, the process should not detract from the core business of working with young children – that of extending their learning, interacting and offer appropriate challenge and support. As the EYFS Statutory Framework section 2.2 clearly states: 'Assessment should not entail prolonged breaks from interaction with children nor require excessive paperwork. Paperwork should be limited to that which is absolutely necessary to promote children's successful learning and development.' A fourth key principle is the need to involve families in the observation, assessment and planning process – not as passive 'receivers' of a summative assessment at key stages. It is worth revisiting Principles into Practice card 3.1 (DCSF 2008), which reminds us that the child should be the starting point for all observation, assessment and planning, and that families should be involved:

Starting with the Child

- observe children to find out about their needs, what they are interested in and what they can do
- note children's responses in different situations
- analyse your observation and highlight children's achievements or their need for further support
- involve parents as part of the ongoing observation and assessment process.

If these four key principles are kept to the forefront, everything else should fall into place. Practitioners should not be led by formats and paperwork, and observations should certainly not be content driven. If practitioners in the reception year are expected to provide a 'short commentary' at the end of the reception year for Year 1 teachers, then this must be good practice *throughout* the EYFS. One of the findings from the EYFS Profile pilot undertaken in summer 2012, in preparation for the revisions in 2013, was that many reception class teachers actually found this commentary the most challenging to complete. We clearly have some way to go if we, as a workforce, are so bound up in the content of *what* children are learning that we have no clear picture or overview of *how* they are learning.

If we are to be able to give a clear summary of how children are learning, then observations of how they are learning need to be core to everyday practice. Some local authorities are giving a strong steer on the importance of this. Wokingham Borough Council, for example, developed pro formas and guidance for their 'I am two: what I can do' summary, in response to the introduction of the Progress Check at Two. A cross-professional working group identified that the Progress Check at Two should include not only the three prime areas, but also a commentary on the characteristics of effective learning. Moreover, 'I am Two' has become part of a suite of materials supporting practitioners throughout the EYFS, offering guidance for summative assessment, based on observation, until the end of the reception year.

The materials all emphasize the importance of a summary of the characteristics of effective learning as well as including families in the process. For example, the information for parents about 'I am Two' includes the following:

I am a Unique Child: I am Two – What I can do

A time to share:

When your child is between the ages of two and three years you will be invited as the parent/carer to celebrate what your child can do both at home and in the setting.

Although this invitation to share information at this stage in your child's life is a requirement for the setting, we need your support to complete it.

The information that we share will complement and sit alongside the two year review you are likely to have with your Health Visitor.

We would like you to tell us:

- What your child likes doing.
- What your child is learning or has just learnt.
- Any new words/sentences, or new ways of communicating.
- Particular interests and fascinations.
- The ways your child explores, learns and plays.
- Anything else you want to share about your child.

Observing

If observations of the child are at the heart of the observation, assessment and planning process, we need to consider how this works in practice. Practitioners may use many formats for recording what they see and hear children doing. Some of these observations may be long, planned observations and, as is increasingly popular, many may be 'spontaneous', short observations of key moments of significant achievement.

But sometimes we are so focused on 'learning intentions', that we miss the key, significant learning that is going on all around us. We may be so busy 'observing' how children are ordering numbers from zero to ten, as they peg number cards they have made onto a washing line as part of an adult planned experience, that we fail to observe how they are approaching the process. So we may miss:

Flavia: Piling the number cards up, then collecting another set from the maths learning zone and matching the numerals – putting a '2' with a '2' and a '3' with a '3'. Then shuffling all the cards and dealing them out to friends.

Serge: Sorting the cards into piles of 'even' and 'odd' numbers – counting in twos out loud. Walking away, still chanting 'two, four, six, eight, who do we appreciate?'

Charlotte: Singing 'Ten in a Bed' as she fixes the cards to the line, and calling to Charlene 'come and play 10 in a bed with me, bring the babies'. Spending over twenty minutes pegging up the cards, laying them in a row and matching one toy to each, singing and laughing.

Rifat: Struggling with using the pegs to fix the cards onto the washing line. Looking hard at the pegs, practising opening and closing them with two hands, and watching other children. Then having another go and beaming as the card remains fixed to the line.

Milo: Refusing to join in with the activity when invited by the practitioner, but later returning, when the adult and group of children leave. Looking at the cards, and fixing the '4' card onto the line – between the '7' and '8', saying 'Four, I four'.

So in focusing so narrowly on the planned learning intentions, a practitioner could miss significant learning in other areas of learning and development – Rifat's physical development, Charlotte's development in the expressive arts, Serge's personal, social and emotional development. What's more, really important information about *how* children learn could be missed too. If we look harder, we can see that we could make comments about the children's approaches to learning:

Flavia: The way that Flavia is thinking and learning – *'having her own ideas'* about how to use the resource and putting them into practice **(creating and thinking critically)**.

Serge: The way Serge is thinking and *'making links'* in his learning – how he is thinking about the oral 'counting in twos' activity earlier in the week **(creating and thinking critically)**.

Charlotte: The way Charlotte continues to be *motivated* by a task she sets herself – how she is *'involved and concentrating'* for a prolonged period **(active learning)**.

Rifat: The way Rifat exhibits his *motivation* – how he *'keeps on trying'* and *'enjoys achieving what he sets out to do'* **(active learning)**.

Milo: The way Milo becomes *engaged* in the experience, after initial reluctance – being willing to *'have a go'* away from the group **(playing and exploring)**.

So practitioners who are really watching and listening to children, with eyes wide open and ears alert, can find out a lot about *how* they are learning as well as what they are learning, as long as flexibility is intrinsic to the ethos of the setting. They can see *how* children are playing and exploring **(engagement)**, learning actively **(motivation)** and creating and thinking critically **(thinking)** – in short, how they exhibit being 'ready, willing and able' to learn.

It is worth reflecting on the fascinating 'Invisible Gorilla' experiment (Chabris and Simons 2011). In the original video footage, observers are asked to focus on a particular task – counting the number of basketball passes. Part way through the game, a person in a gorilla costume walks onto the court, and off again. About half of all observers are so focused on their task of counting, that they completely miss the 'gorilla'. We too, can be so focused on what we want, or expect to observe, that we fail to notice the *real* learning going on throughout the indoor and outdoor provision. We need to remember the importance of:

- Observing children as a natural part of all normal activity
- Interpreting children's actions and words to try to understand the child's thinking and learning
- Being sensitive to the child's thinking and learning when deciding when to interact and when to value the child's independent activity
- Joining in play and child-initiated activity following children's agendas
- Scaffolding children's learning through talk, discussing strategies and ideas, suggesting possibilities and modelling approaches
- Providing brief, well-planned focused learning opportunities in response to observed interests, learning and development

(DCSF 2009: 27)

When we respond to children's independent activities, and accept their invitations to become co-players, we become engrossed in participant observations and notice significant events:

Sebastian: We will see how Sebastian notices the markings on a pebble, and sets out to make a collection of pebbles in a bucket, involving adults and peers, digging in the outside area. We will find out how he is showing curiosity about objects; using his senses to explore the world around him; initiating activities; maintaining focus for a period of time; not easily distracted; finding new ways to do things and making decisions about how to approach a task – **finding out and exploring, choosing ways to do things** and **enjoying what he sets out to do.**

Remi: We will notice that although Remi first gets really upset that the tower of empty boxes he is building collapses, he goes on to learn from his early attempts, draws in peers and develops ways to build a stable base, starting again several times until he succeeds. We'll notice that he then moves onto constructing with crates outdoors, and applies what he has learnt there too. We will find out how he is showing particular interests; seeking challenge; showing a 'can do' attitude; paying attention to details; persisting when challenges occur; bouncing back after difficulties; finding ways to solve problems and changing strategy as needed – **finding out and exploring, choosing ways to do things** and **enjoying what he sets out to do.**

Rima: We will notice that Rima collects some empty boxes from the creative workshop, gathers up wrapping paper, string and ribbons and struggles with different ways to wrap 'parcels', making labels. We will see when she gestures and invites friends to a 'party' and sets up a picnic on the grass outdoors – playing 'pass the parcel' and 'musical bumps'. We will find out how she is acting out experiences with other people; taking on a role in her play; learning by trial and error; maintaining focus on an activity for a period of time; showing high levels of energy and fascination; thinking of ideas and reviewing how well an approach is working – **finding out and exploring, choosing ways to do things** and **enjoying what she sets out to do.**

Practitioners who create a learning environment which values *how* children learn as well as *what* they are learning will be able to make meaningful, significant observations which will support effective assessment and impact on ongoing planning.

Assessing

Assessment is all about reflecting on observations and other knowledge of a child to decide what it means in terms of the child's interests, current focus of learning, ways of thinking, emotional response and level of development. Quite simply, assessment involves the practitioner making an informed judgement about the child's learning.

The EYFS Statutory Framework (DfE 2012b) requires early years practitioners to review children's progress and share a summary with parents at two points: in the prime areas between the ages of 24 and 36 months (the Progress Check at Age Two), and at the end of the EYFS (the EYFS Profile).

> Assessment plays an important part in helping parents, carers and practitioners to recognise children's progress, understand their needs, and to plan activities and support. Ongoing assessment (also known as formative assessment) is an integral part of the learning and development process. It involves practitioners observing children to understand their level of achievement, interests and learning styles, and to then shape learning experiences for each child reflecting those observations. In their interactions with children, practitioners should respond to their own day-to-day observations about children's progress, and observations that parents and carers share.
>
> (DfE 2012b: 2.1)

Statutory assessment

Progress Check at Age Two

When a child is aged between 2 and 3, practitioners must review their progress and provide parents and/or carers with a short written summary of their child's development in the prime areas.

Beyond the prime areas, it is for practitioners to decide what the written summary should include, reflecting the development level and needs of the individual child (DfE 2012b: 2.3 and 2.4).

The National Children's Bureau non-statutory guidance explains that the progress check:

- should be completed by a practitioner who knows the child well and works directly with them in the setting. This should normally be the child's key person
- arises from the ongoing observational assessments carried out as part of everyday practice in the setting
- is based on skills, knowledge, understanding and behaviour that the child demonstrates consistently and independently
- takes account of the views and contributions of parents
- takes into account the views of other practitioners and, where relevant, other professionals working with the child
- enables children to contribute actively to the process.

(NCB 2012: 3)

Although there is no statutory obligation to include a commentary on the characteristics of effective learning in the Progress Check at Age Two, one example shared in the non-statutory guidance, from the Early Learning Consultancy (NCB 2012: 27), includes such a commentary, as do many local authority examples, including the Wokingham Borough Council 'I am Two' document (see page 95 above).

An informative paragraph, written in collaboration with parents, will capture the essence of the way in which a child is learning as a 'snapshot' at some time between the ages of 24 and 36 months. For example:

I am Unique – Shaun

Playing and exploring
Finding out and exploring; playing with what they know; being willing to 'have a go'

Active learning
Being involved and concentrating; enjoying achieving what they set out to do; keeping on trying

Creating and thinking critically
Having their own ideas; making links; choosing ways to do things

Shaun is very eager to explore all the centre provision – moving between being indoors and outdoors. He has a real 'can do' attitude and loves to challenge his physical abilities – he recently discovered how to hop after watching older children and persisted until he could use both legs. One of Shaun's favourite activities is painting with water and large brushes. He really engages in this open-ended activity and maintains focus for long periods. He finds the water butt tap difficult to turn on, but really persists.

I am Unique – Carla

Playing and exploring
Finding out and exploring; playing with what they know; being willing to 'have a go'

Active learning
Being involved and concentrating; enjoying achieving what they set out to do; keeping on trying

Creating and thinking critically
Having their own ideas; making links; choosing ways to do things

Carla really likes small things – she picks them up and trickles them between her fingers. When she is outdoors she loves to make collections of twigs, pebbles and leaves. Most recently she likes to put these in a particular saucepan and stir with a wooden spoon from the home corner. She has begun to offer favourite friends and her key person 'dinner', pretending the leaves and twigs are food and taking on roles in her play. Carla is very eager to take off and put on her own clothes – and persists even when her shoes are difficult to put back on.

Early Years Foundation Stage Profile

The EYFS Profile (DfE 2012a) is completed in the final term of the year in which the child reaches age 5, and no later than 30 June in that term. The profile provides parents and carers, practitioners and teachers with a well-rounded picture of a child's knowledge, understanding and abilities. In addition to an assessment for each of the 17 early learning goals (ELGs) in which practitioners must indicate whether children are meeting expected levels of development, or if they are exceeding expected levels, or not yet reaching expected levels ('emerging'), practitioners must also provide a short commentary on each child's skills and abilities in relation to the three key characteristics of effective learning.

The most useful commentary about the characteristics of effective learning will summarize the way a child learns within the school, but also reflect parental views of how the child is learning at home. When families have been involved in discussions about *how* their child is learning throughout the EYFS, they will be well placed to contribute in a meaningful way.

Chaz, 4 years 11 months

EYFS: characteristics of effective learning

Playing and exploring
Finding out and exploring; playing with what they know; being willing to 'have a go'

Chaz has a particular interest in outdoor play. Most recently he loves to take on the role of 'Merlin', initiating activities and drawing his friends into his play, acting out their experiences in their play. He uses branches as 'wands' and makes collections of natural objects for magic potions, pretending these objects are magical items.

Active learning
Being involved and concentrating; enjoying achieving what they set out to do; keeping on trying

Chaz focuses on preferred activities for long periods of time and is not easily engaged by adults when he is choosing to 'mix potions', 'cast spells' or planning 'rescue missions' across the climbing frame and in the wooded area. Chaz sets challenges for himself and others – most recently using the tyres, blankets and logs to create 'stepping stones' across a 'river'. He really persists with these self-identified challenges and shows great satisfaction in meeting his own goals.

Creating and thinking critically
Having their own ideas; making links; choosing ways to do things

Chaz is beginning to make links in his learning. Most recently he was trying to move a builders' bucket filled with wet mud. He couldn't move it on his own, and actually sat down and looked for a few minutes before emptying some of the mud into a box. He moved the bucket and refilled – predicting what would happen, trying out his idea and solving his problem. Later he used a different strategy – asking his friend to help him put the bucket on the wheeled toy to move it.

Mei-Xing, 5 years 8 months

EYFS: characteristics of effective learning

Playing and exploring
Finding out and exploring; playing with what they know; being willing to 'have a go'

Mei-Xing engages in a wide range of activities, both indoors and outdoors. She has a particular interest in role play and imaginative play. Mei-Xing spends a lot of time being 'mum', using dolls as her twins sisters and engaging her two close friends H and K-L in her play themes. Mei-Xing is very interested in people – she loves visitors and always approaches them with confidence, asking questions about their family, where they live and what they do.

Active learning
Being involved and concentrating; enjoying achieving what they set out to do; keeping on trying

Mei-Xing is fascinated by small things and particularly likes to find tiny things in the dry sand – she sieves for nuggets and 'treasure' and use tweezers to move items into treasure boxes, sometimes focusing on this activity for prolonged periods. Mei-Xing pays attention to very small details when involved in one of her passions – fixing shiny, glittery objects onto small pieces of card to create greetings cards. She recently found out how to make a 'pop-up' card and persisted, even when she found the cutting for the hinge challenging. When she cut right across the card first time, she used masking tape to fix the card and was extremely satisfied when the card opened and 'popped up'.

Creating and thinking critically
Having their own ideas; making links; choosing ways to do things.

Mei-Xing spends long periods watching other children when they are doing something new and unusual. She often takes an idea and innovates – for example, making a 'double zig-zag' book when her story about her family was too long for eight pictures. She tried out her idea for the book first and only fixed it when she was sure it would work. She then showed her best friend H how to make the book. When she tried to make a stapled book and realized it wouldn't work, she approached C, her key person, for support. She knew she couldn't use masking tape for all the pages and worked with C for a long time, eventually making a 'staple-less' book together.

Planning

> No plan written weeks in advance can include a group's interest in a spider's web on a frosty morning or a particular child's interest in transporting small objects in a favourite blue bucket, yet it is these interests which may lead to some powerful learning. Plans should therefore be flexible enough to adapt to circumstances.
>
> (DCSF 2008: 12)

Planning involves deciding what to provide next to support the child's learning, informed by what the practitioner finds out about the child from the assessment process. Effective planning includes a wide range of ways of interacting through which practitioners can support and extend learning.
Effective planning should:

- ensure children are excited to learn and effectively supported;
- identify opportunities to explore ideas, resources, experiences;
- be developmentally appropriate;
- provide a tool kit for adults – but be enabling not restrictive.

As long ago as 2001, the QCA emphasized the need to identify *how* children learn:

> [C]hildren who begin their education in a learning environment that is vibrant, purposeful, challenging and supportive stand the best chance of developing into confident and successful learners. Effective learning environments are created over time as a result of practitioners and parents working together, thinking and talking about children's learning and planning how to promote it. Good planning is the key to making children's learning effective, exciting, varied and progressive. Good planning enables practitioners to build up knowledge about *how* individual children learn and make progress. It also provides opportunities for practitioners to think and talk about how to sustain a successful learning environment.
>
> (QCA 2001: 2, original emphasis)

Practitioners need to ensure coverage of the seven areas of learning and development over a period of time. But what is absolutely essential is planning to create a rich, vibrant learning environment which supports children's own interests and supports the characteristics of effective learning: an indoor and outdoor environment which motivates and engages children and supports the ways in which they think, helping them to develop their own 'tool kit' for learning.

A well-planned environment should include the following:

- Open-ended, accessible resources which can be used in a variety of diverse ways – for example, two sets of wooden blocks of different sizes, which fit together, will offer children more options than a complex construction kit which can only be fitted together in one way.
- Resources which reflect children's current interests and enthusiasms – if a group are fascinated by superheroes, support this interest through open-ended resources which can be used as cloaks, or provide superhero comics and images.
- Spaces which can be used in different ways, so that children can make links within their learning. Rigidly defined areas can be limiting. For example, provide rugs, duvet covers and blankets which children can use indoors and outdoors to define their own learning areas and spaces.
- Quiet spaces, which are visually calm. Limit noise by keeping adult voices low, rather than speaking over children. Make sure children have lots of space and time outdoors to be loud and physical, but also quiet, serene spaces outdoors.
- Familiar, favourite resources but also, on a regular basis, novel and unusual resources to investigate and explore, particularly those linked to their current interests.
- Resources which arouse children's curiosity and intrinsically motivate children, promoting deep involvement.

- Flexible routines which ensure children have opportunities to become deeply involved – no more stopping playing to 'go out to play'.
- Opportunities for children to revisit activities over a period of time. For example, where possible, the flexibility of leaving large constructions out to be developed over days, rather than 'tidied up' every session.

Adult-initiated activities

As the EYFS Statutory Framework states, 'There is an ongoing judgement to be made by practitioners about the balance between activities led by children, and activities led or guided by adults' (DfE 2012b: 1.9).

> Adult-initiated activities build on children's current interests. However they are also planned because familiar adults have good reasons to expect that this experience will engage the children. Young children cannot ask to do something again, or develop their own version, until they have that first time experience. The best plans are flexible; there is scope for the children to influence the details and adults can respond to what actually happens.
>
> (Stevens 2012: 2)

When planning adult-initiated experiences, practitioners need to ensure that activities motivate and engage children – open activities will offer children more opportunities to find their own ways to represent and develop their own ideas, not simply reproducing someone else's ideas.

The Cambridgeshire Independent Learning Project (C.Ind.Le; Whitebread et al. 2008, see Chapter 2 of this volume) found examples of children showing characteristics of effective learning in all sorts of contexts, but they identified that they were most common in certain situations, in particular:

- children initiating activities (setting personally meaningful goals and challenges);
- opportunities to work in unsupervised groups (self-directed learning; resolving problems for themselves);
- extensive collaboration and talk (visible learning; making strategies and decisions explicit).

Practitioners, then, should reflect on the daily opportunities children have to engage in these sorts of activities. Effective planning should include specific examples of things adults could do (positive relationships) and provide (enabling environments), having made particular observations of the ways in which individual children are currently learning.

Consider then, the approach practitioners take to planning adult-initiated activities for a small group of children. One common approach may be to plan a specific activity, which offers opportunities for assessment. The practitioner plans an activity, based on observations of the children, identifying a learning intention of *'Counts up to three or four objects by saying one number name for each item'*. Building on the children's interests in rhymes, the practitioners provides five green speckled frogs, a log and some crepe paper 'lily pad' leaves. The children engage in counting the frogs, some counting three or four frogs, saying one number name for each. The children are engaged, the practitioner makes observations and assesses their achievement in that particular aspect of learning and development.

But consider the limitations of the activity, and how these could be avoided. If the children are fascinated by the number rhyme 'Five Little Speckled Frogs', then make a collection of all sorts of frogs – wooden, fabric, plastic, in different shapes, sizes and colours. Introduce these in wicker baskets, alongside logs and natural objects. Observe how the children investigate and explore the resources. Note how they 'count up to three or four objects by saying one number name for each item', but notice so much more as well. The observations will show not only the children's achievements in one aspect of mathematics but *how* they solve mathematical problems they have identified themselves, and *how* they are learning:

Sabiha: Notice the descriptive and comparative language Sabiha uses as she sorts the frogs. Notice the words she uses to compare the size of the sets she creates 'there are more green frogs, there's millions. No, not millions, one, two, three . . . eleven.' Notice also, how she puts the frogs into sets, starting with materials, then realizing this is too complex, debates size and moves on to colour – green, and 'not green'. She *plans, makes decisions about how to approach her self-identified task, solves the problem and reaches her goal.*

Eddie: Notice how Eddie lines the frogs up and counts them, then how he throws them all in the air and tries to count them where they land. When he gets to 'seven', notice his *satisfaction*: 'That's my brother, that is – seven. I be seven too after Christmas.' Notice too how he *makes predictions* and *keeps on trying, showing a belief that a different approach will pay off.*

Each of these approaches to adult-initiated activities will give practitioners opportunities to observe and assess children's achievement in numbers, but one, in its rigidity, may limit children's achievements, and one will offer opportunities for children to exhibit what they know and can do, and how they are learning. The richness of the observations will feed into more accurate assessments and provide deeper insight which will lead to more effective planning.

Planning to enhance provision

Observations of the ways in which children are learning, in specific areas of continuous provision, will impact on the ways in which practitioners plan to enhance the provision. For example, practitioners can support children as they are 'playing with what they know' in the home corner.

Some examples of what adults could provide **(enabling environments)**:

- Provide well organized, accessible, open-ended resources which can be used in different ways. Instead of a plastic iron, plastic cups, a battery-operated pop-up toaster and purpose-made dressing up clothes, add collections of 'real' kitchen utensils – spoons, ladles, barbecue equipment. Add lengths of interesting fabrics like camouflage materials, sheer fabric, netting, shiny and textured fabrics. Or consider adding a collection of shoes and shoe boxes, or hats for a short while.
- Fix a digital photo frame to the wall, with a slide show of children's real experiences – when they visited the farm and the supermarket; when the firefighters, Sally's mum and the baby came to the settings and 'animal man' visited; when they went on a number walk around the local area. Keep the slide show up to date *with* the children. Display still images of different homes.

Some examples of what adults could do **(positive relationships)**:

- Act as a co-player with the children in the home corner, sensitively fitting in with their ideas and play themes. Take on a role – as disgruntled teenager, busy mum, or granny visiting from overseas. Act out your own experiences and support them to act out theirs.
- Use an object in unfamiliar ways, pretending it is something else – use a box as a bucket to mop the floor, or as a crib for a baby. Use a block as an iPad, games console or mobile phone – showing what it is by the way it is being used.
- Support children without taking over their play – if they are playing at 'being Uncle Elijah', make comments about what they are doing or, where appropriate, ask open questions to extend the play 'I'm making pancakes for tea because they are my favourite. Do you have a favourite cake, Uncle?'

In summary then, this chapter has explored why and how we need to remember to:

- keep the child at the heart of the observation, assessment and planning process;
- avoid mountains of paperwork and note children's significant learning – including *how* they are learning and use this to inform planning;
- spend as much time as possible interacting with children, acting as co-players, offering challenge and extending their learning;
- involve families in the process in meaningful ways – in particular how children are learning at home and their current fascinations.

References

Chabris, C. and Simons, D. (2011) *The Invisible Gorilla.* New York: HarperCollins.

DCSF (Department for Children, Schools and Families) (2008) *The Early Years Foundation Stage.* www.foundationyears.org.uk/category/library/publications/ (accessed 15 December 2012).

DCSF (Department for Children, Schools and Families) (2009) *Learning, Playing and Interacting: Good Practice in the Early Years Foundation Stage,* 00775-2009BKT-EN. http://www.foundationyears.org.uk/category/library/national-strategies-resources/page/11/ (accessed 22 December 2012).

DfE (2012a) *Early Years Foundation Stage Profile Handbook 2013.* http://www.foundationyears.org.uk/early-years-foundation-stage-2012/(accessed 20 December 2012).

DfE (Department for Education) (2012b) *Statutory Framework for the Early Years Foundation Stage: Setting the Standards for Learning, Development and Care for Children from Birth to Five.* http://www.foundationyears.org.uk/early-years-foundation-stage-2012/ or www.education.gov.uk/aboutdfe/statutory/g00213120/eyfs-statutory-framework (accessed 1 January 2013).

Early Education (2012) *Development Matters in the Early Years Foundation Stage.* London: Early Education. www.early-education.org.uk and for download at http://www.foundationyears.org.uk/early-years-foundation-stage-2012/ (accessed 20 December 2012).

NCB (National Children's Bureau) (2012) *A Know How Guide: The EYFS Progress Check at Age Two.* http://www.foundationyears.org.uk/early-years-foundation-stage-2012/ (accessed 22 December 2012).

QCA (2001) *Planning for Learning in the Foundation Stage.* London: QCA. https://www.education.gov.uk/publications/eOrderingDownload/QCA-01-799.pdf.pdf (accessed 20 December 2012).

Stevens, J. (2012) *Planning for the Early Years: Storytelling and Storymaking.* London: Practical Preschool Books.

Whitebread, D. with Dawkins, R., Bingham, S., Aguda, A. and Hemming, K. (2008) Organising the early years classroom to encourage independent learning, in D. Whitebread and P. Coltman (eds) *Teaching and Learning in the Early Years*, 3rd edn. London: Routledge.

7 Exploring the development of a learning community at Norland Nursery

Clare Crowther

The term 'learning community' has been commonplace in schools for some time and has recently become more widespread in early years. The term encompasses a range of practices, often visible within, or facilitated through, the daily provision at an early years centre. This may include parent information groups and making use of the wider community through visits or it may be seen through the reflective conversations held between staff during supervision sessions.

In an early years context, the term 'professional learning community' often summarizes the engagement of all stakeholders in enhancing the learning opportunities of children, their parents and the staff working alongside them. It describes the variety of ways in which early years practitioners, parents and children work and learn together. With the current political and economic focus, and the changing landscape of early years provision, it seems important as a sector to affirm our understanding of the roles we hold in creating, maintaining and facilitating the learning communities we belong to and lead.

In this chapter I explore the development of the learning community at Norland Nursery and the shaping influence it has upon our practice and the services we offer. The characteristics of effective learning (the skill, will and thrill of learning for children and adults) have played a key role in our continuing journey of development and change.

Case study of Norland Nursery

Norland Nursery opened in the summer of 2009. The nursery offers full-day care and is registered for 61 children aged from 16 weeks to 5 years. The vision of the nursery is to offer the highest level of care together with the richest opportunities for learning for babies and young children.

The staff team at Norland Nursery have been encouraged to use their personal and professional learning to reflect upon their practice with children and families, in order to enhance the philosophy of the setting. The philosophy has the work of Froebel as its foundations, is influenced by a range of other educationalists and theorists and has found itself 'standing on the shoulders of giants' (Whalley 2011) such as Vygotsky, Malaguzzi, Athey and Laevers.

All of the above have informed a successful pedagogy that includes a free flow, workshop approach and an emotionally enabling environment, in which children are cared for in mixed age key family groupings.

In implementing the philosophy of the nursery several significant challenges arose for the team as recognition of the physical, emotional and cognitive demands of working in this chosen way were revealed. Staff needed the opportunity to challenge, debate, question and reflect upon the ways in which they were being asked to work – and thus our professional learning community began to emerge.

Education pioneer Chris Athey discusses the basis for constructivism, and, in my view, the underpinning principle of a professional learning community when she states: 'The main value of Froebelian Pedagogy and "Constructivism", the main system of educational research endeavours of the last century, is quite simple. It is based on the conviction that each individual learner contributes to and collaborates in, his or her own learning' (2004: 11).

Influenced by Athey it became clear that contribution and collaboration between

- staff member and staff member
- staff member and parent
- staff and children
- parents and children

were required for all stakeholders to have ownership of the pedagogy and to enhance their own and others' learning. The responsibility of facilitating such relationships would initially fall to myself as leader of the setting.

It is well recognized that the role of a leader in establishing a learning community is complex. The leader is required to determine strategies, processes and procedures that enable the vision to be successfully implemented, thus there is a need to take a multi-dimensional approach (Jorde-Bloom 1992: 138).

The role of the leader in developing a learning community

The leader is often seen as being the one responsible for creating and maintaining the vision and ethos of the centre, but I do not see this as only my individual effort. Striving to create a learning community, I felt it important that each member of the team was able to work collaboratively in the process of creating and maintaining our vision, and that my role would be to facilitate and champion this.

So, when considering the vision for the nursery, we not only used theory together with international, national and local practice to shape our thoughts. We also took time to reflect upon our own personal and professional experiences and the core values we held as individuals and as a team.

Our reflections and research led us to focus upon key elements of our provision; key elements that as a learning community we continue to explore and embed in our practice. These include:

- the quality of our provision; questioning what quality looks like in practice; how it is to be maintained and how it will be evaluated;
- the inclusion of children and families at the nursery with genuine recognition of their context and circumstances;
- the forming of genuine relationships and how best to ensure emotional security, respect, equality and empowerment;
- how to ensure democracy across all stakeholders;
- the pedagogy of the nursery, how our babies and young children learn best and most effectively and how we resource this;
- the recognition and promotion of the characteristics of learning both for children and ourselves, with the question of how we were going to ensure the 'skill, will and thrill' of learning for all involved in order to make it easier for children to be active, playful, creative thinkers and learners.

As with most teams, the staff members have a diverse range of skills, knowledge and understanding. Recognizing this and with the key elements of practice in continual debate, implementing the vision of the nursery required a range of leadership styles. The selected styles needed to be flexible and responsive to the context as well as being supportive and shared and I needed to ensure I promoted both transformational and distributive leadership (Law and Glover 2000).

The sharing of leadership, power and decision making

This was, at times, a very challenging process. The aim was the development of a collegial relationship with the staff team which would empower and enable staff, which in turn would empower and enable the children and their families. This heterarchical approach (Marshall 1994) recognizes the peaks of leadership required across the varying aspects of our practice and the services we wished to offer.

However it also challenged some members of the team, who on the whole had only experienced a traditional management style, leading to a hierarchical view of the headteacher being omnicompetent – 'all wise and all competent'. This led to some hesitation when staff were given the option of being encouraged to question and challenge those holding a more senior role, in order to make meaning and seek solutions both for themselves as individuals and also for the wider team.

Gradually a new relationship began to be forged in which everyone was able to contribute. Staff grew professionally and began to view themselves as leaders in their own right, who were all working towards the same vision: to provide the highest quality of care and education to the children and their families. A culture began to develop characterized by involvement, openness and trust. The characteristics we wanted for the children in our care were now present for the staff. They felt a sense of belonging and were self-regulated learners in their own right.

The empowerment of staff increased as leaders of the team sought 'power for' as opposed to 'power over' the staff team (Whalley 2006). From this shift in thinking and working came an appreciation that shared power was about having an ability to make things happen. Staff became increasingly committed to the children as well as to each other and to education – they were committed to collaboration.

Whalley (2007) discusses the learning community created at the Pen Green Centre as an environment in which:

- children, parents and staff were encouraged to be good decision makers, able to question, challenge and make choices;
- there were opportunities for staff to become highly trained, reflective practitioners with good levels of support and supervision, in an environment where they could build satisfactory relationships and feel valued personally and professionally;
- staff consulted and felt comfortable with all stakeholders – children, parents, staff, the community, the local authority;
- parents had become advocates for their children and were beginning to share in their understanding of their children's learning at home and with nursery staff.

It was these elements that began to evolve at the nursery but I was aware that staff needed to underpin these beginnings by becoming constructive in their ability to challenge practices and, as such, further develop their own ability to think creatively.

Cultivating creativity among the staff team

The concept of a learning community in which people's new thinking is nurtured and aspirations set free, is a shift from the traditional paradigm. However, many early years settings are now establishing a culture in which people come together to learn and to test ideas and processes in order to create the outcomes they desire both for the children and for the wider setting. It was this guardianship of learning, together with nurturing of new thinking, which I wished to promote.

I am aware that as a team we strive to enable and empower the children in their learning. We offer an award-winning learning environment rich in resources, to motivate children in following their personal agenda. Staff work alongside the children in their play, making sensitive observations, prior to carefully planning for them, with their behaviours demonstrating that they are eager to support children in their explorations, acting as researchers alongside the children (Malaguzzi 1993) (see for example, Crowther 2012a, b and c). Our observations of children working in this way affirm our belief that our holistic approach of planning for the child, as opposed to planning for the curriculum, enables children to become self-regulated learners. We identify children's levels of well-being and involvement (Laevers 1997) as being high, with children active in their learning.

It is the same cultivation of creative thinking that I have endeavoured to instil among the nursery staff team, while seeking to generate a sense of excitement and enthusiasm for learning that fosters both engagement and satisfaction.

The encouragement of staff to hold high aspirations for themselves and to take responsibility for their own learning has naturally led to staff questioning how they can improve their practice, increase their knowledge and develop their professional understandings. Answers to these questions are explored either through reflective conversations during supervision sessions or alternatively through small focus groups in which staff participate in transparent dialogue.

Developing a culture of open dialogue

The joys and challenges of establishing such a learning community have been vast, with the maintainence of such a way of working requiring energy, focus, enthusiasm and above all, communication. The learning community at the nursery has seen communication strategies evolve to form a culture in which challenging others and questioning practice are acceptable.

A sense of ownership has been created and a clear understanding and rationale for our practice and a valuing of the work we undertake now fully exist through open and transparent dialogue. With stakeholders at all levels participating within the learning community, members seek to work together collaboratively, supported by their reflective conversations.

This open and honest dialogue forces debate within a safe environment, which in turn promotes enquiry, understanding and appreciation of others. It assists the binding of the team in meeting our aims, in accepting the challenges we face and in seeking shared solutions and ownership.

One informal strategy is the use of 'Conversational Café' (Robbins 2001). It promotes experiential learning (Kolb 1995) and provides a holistic model of a learning process which is consistent with the ways in which we see children learn most effectively. Conversational Café is the simplest of strategies and takes the form of a non-agenda informal meeting. Staff are invited to participate, rather than required to. Interestingly, the voluntary nature of the experience has immediately led to higher levels of involvement from staff than those seen in formal meetings. The environment is set up to feel relaxed and physically comfortable – use of a neutral space and consideration as to the timing of the café promote staff well-being and a sense of value.

A discussion topic may be decided prior to the meeting, thus determining those who wish to be involved. Alternatively, regular cafés take place that offer opportunity to discuss more generic issues such as the development of learning spaces, or the implementation of policy and procedure as well as our responses to the pressures, critical incidents or learning currently taking place within the nursery.

The use of iPads and social media acts as a springboard for political debate or to research and add further dimension to the conversation. For example when the Nutbrown report on the Early Years Workforce (Nutbrown 2012) was released the nursery staff team made use of social media to gain others' perceptions of the findings and recommendations which in turn enabled a reflective dialogue during a conversational café. This process empowered the staff to determine their thoughts and submit their views to leading publications. These statements are referred to often and have led to further conversations regarding the role of the early years professional.

Team members participating within conversational café and reflective conversations are able to seek affirmation and solution. They are able to create new pathways of thinking, within shared practice, creatively approaching their work while maintaining the vision and shared values of the nursery. They play with ideas and explore ways forward, creating and thinking critically at their own level as well as showing the skills involved in active learning – deep involvement and concentration as well as persistence and enjoyment in their own achievements.

Implementing the ethos and embedding it in practice

The goals of what we are attempting to achieve needed to be managed. It is well recognized that successful teams are characterized by a set of achievable goals that are understood and accepted by all (Rodd 2010). As part of the process of becoming a true learning community, the wider vision needed to be broken down into smaller, much more achievable, tasks for both the staff team and also for the families who were accessing our centre.

We needed to review the principles of what we were trying to achieve and the policies that were guiding our operation. We began with the core elements of our ethos to ensure that as a team the foundations of our practice were strong and embedded before adding further dimensions to our work.

It was recognized that the core elements we needed to focus upon were going to be:

- the key person approach and mixed age key families;
- the learning environment;
- the routines of the children.

In focusing upon these, the *personal* ideas and values of staff members quickly surfaced and it became apparent that they exerted as great an influence upon the formation of our practice as the *professional* value system that we held.

Recognizing that it was not uncommon to have conflict between staff in their aims for children (Vander Ven 1988) it became imperative to explore the personal and professional expectations of team members in terms of behaviour, children's needs, educational processes, working with parents, and the organization of the nursery and learning environment. As a leader I was able to clarify the professional values but needed to ensure that the personal values were articulated and explored in order to prevent unnecessary conflict from occurring.

Complex decisions needed to be made as to how the identified core elements of our practice were to develop. The team was rich in qualification but limited in professional experience and maturity. This in turn led to an understandable sense among the staff of feeling overwhelmed, which often led to a response of 'Please, just tell us what to do'.

The need to search for a solution both in our core practices and for the team could easily have led to the construction of a solution based on past experiences or familiar alternatives (Hasenfield 1983). This, however, would not have enabled the innovative thinking of those implementing the ethos. So, instead, a creative approach to problem solving was hosted that led to a range of new ideas being presented by team members. Working in this way allowed the bigger picture to be seen with staff encouraged to actively take informed risks to try out new strategies. Below, three of my colleagues talk about what some of this process means to them.

> When we first opened, I couldn't really see how the mixed ages would work, the babies were disturbing the older children's learning and I just couldn't accept that the babies would be safe if they were allowed to move throughout the nursery. I really struggled that we didn't have our own specific rooms with a specific age of child to look after. However, now having worked through all of the processes and seeing that it can work I would never change what we do, the children are able to make their own choices, and decisions, they learn from each other and cooperate together. It's a much more exciting way of working for both the children and us.

It has been a really steep learning curve for me since I joined Norland, there is a really high expectation, but it's good, really good, because we are always doing the best for the children and the families. There aren't many nurseries that allow you to take your key family to London at the weekend to view an art exhibition and encourage you to recreate everything you have seen at the nursery once you get back! I remember it was challenging at first, as I had been taught you needed to have a birthday board, and to use templates, and cut outs, but when I started at Norland it was explained that templates inhibited children's natural creativity, and I was given a range of books to inspire me in the way I worked. Very soon after this, I wanted to host an art exhibition of works completed by the children, based upon a provocation inspired by Andy Goldsworthy and I've never looked back. The ideas I come up with now are led by the children and I'm always supported to explore them.

It's the little things, the everyday things that are really important in what we do. For example the way we need to think about how it feels for the babies, taking notice of what they see and hear. When we were encouraged to see the nursery through the babies' eyes I did think it was a bit mad, but when you lie flat on the floor the world looks like a different place, so it is really important. Sometimes people question why our key person approach is so important, but it's simple to me, I wouldn't want to be changed, fed and put to sleep by a range of different people so why should our babies?

Throughout the initial process (and to this day) I was aware that the quality of decisions we made would impinge upon the quality of work being undertaken and also on the well-being of those implementing the ethos. The role modelling of practice in supporting the staff to develop such full understanding and ownership happened, not just practically on the nursery floor, but perhaps most significantly for the staff team, off the nursery floor during staff planning and non-contact times. In order to implement a rich pedagogy investment in staff time was needed.

Team times and staff non-contact time

Each of five smaller room teams meet once a week to discuss the observations gathered throughout the previous week. These observations can be used to plan for learning opportunities that are purposeful and extend children's knowledge and understanding while also offering opportunities to consolidate prior learning.

Each of these team times is led by a senior member of staff and they act as the pedagogical leaders for the nursery. They hold the role of drawing together all children's experiences, while subtly and seamlessly ensuring all areas of learning and development are promoted. The pedagogical leaders pose questions, prompt debate and offer inspiration and experience. They act as a sounding board for team members, coaching practitioners to deepen their learning and improve provision. For example, when children were observed to be displaying an interest in building and construction their learning was extended in a range of directions through the influence of the pedagogical leader. Staff across the teams planned for opportunities to extend the children's learning. In the technology room children used Google Earth to find their own street and home, discussing the features and properties of their homes before recreating these with the large and small maple blocks. In the discovery room visits and outings were facilitated that took children on an open-top bus tour to view differing types of architecture. The creative room used architectural drawings to inspire model making and design. The story hut in the garden became a building site office, following a visit to the local builders yard and very quickly a pallet of bricks arrived in the garden followed by a visit from a mini digger.

The planning times also allow opportunity for staff to share in their own experiences drawing on the wealth of knowledge within the team thus reinforcing the underpinning principles of the learning community.

Non-contact time for staff is essential. This time allows for refection upon practice, as children's learning journals are completed, and staff are given time to develop themselves professionally either through independent research, further study or participation within a reflective conversation facilitated within a supervision session.

Creating the conditions for a professional learning environment

The non-contact times and staff supervisions have been essential in the success of developing a professional learning community at the nursery. However it quickly became apparent that for the non-contact times to be effective we needed to create the conditions in which staff and families could work comfortably. The physical challenge of getting staff together while respecting their roles and responsibilities during nursery operating hours and while not wanting to impinge upon their personal time or undermine the already high dedication shown to their role, meant that the timing of such meetings required attention.

Staff cohesion

A culture of honest, constructive dialogue developed in which feedback could be offered and received that enabled the team to work towards improvement of the services they offered.

The use of peer video observation has been established as an important staff development tool. Viewed as a collaborative developmental activity from which professionals offer mutual support (Bell 2005) the peer video observations enable staff to develop ideas and gather feedback on their interactions and effectiveness.

Staff were able to work collaboratively in the sharing of ideas and concepts by developing a strong sense of trust, that was initially role modelled to the nursery team by the senior practitioners. Video vignettes were shared within a whole staff meeting for constructive discussion and feedback. The sensitive, yet constructive, handling of video observation demonstrated a respect for others' professional practice and eased staff's initial hesitance to participate. Gradually the reviewing of individual practice, as well as the collective, has become the norm.

Staff have been able to help, support and trust each other as a result of developing caring yet professional working relationships. Staff are now comfortable with each other; they openly share in their successes and weaknesses, offering praise and support in the required measure. They steer away from simply being 'nice' recognizing that, for professional growth to occur, dialogue cannot be based on shallow response. This will at times involve difficult things to say and difficult things to hear but as long as they are shared in a respectful, empathetic and supportive manner this will support the culture to develop further. Staff now seek to continuously share and develop their understanding and learning, holding the view that 'we all have something to offer, we can all get better and together we can achieve our aims'.

The high level of collaboration and mutual respect for each other displayed through the peer observations has been a fundamental requirement in developing learning community practice. We have created 'an environment that values and supports hard work, the acceptance of challenging tasks, risk taking, and the promotion of growth' (Midgley and Wood 1993: 252).

The collegiality has evolved from within the team to encompass the families we are working alongside. There is recognition that for genuine parental partnership to be effective all stakeholders need to be involved in equal measure.

Involving parents in their children's learning

Research and policy inform us that when parents are involved in their children's learning both the children and the parents are likely to benefit. Therefore the next stage in developing and embedding a learning community at the nursery was the full inclusion of parents.

It is reported (Sylva et al. 2004) that parents' participation within children's learning can lead to:

- enhanced self-esteem
- improved achieved and attainment levels
- improved relationships between child and parent
- improved understanding of the educational process and curriculum.

However, in reality the ability to be deeply involved with a child's learning can be challenging. The majority of parents of children attending Norland Nursery juggle hectic work and family lives and so, despite a will to be more involved in their children's learning, time constraints can often prevent a full and purposeful partnership. It therefore became important to us as a team to increase our communication with parents in relation to their children's learning.

Historically, early years settings, including ourselves, participated in parent evenings, parent one-to-one meetings and encouraged parents to spend time in the nursery whenever they could. This in addition to regular newsletters and communication books exploring the child's daily routine was deemed sufficient.

All of these methods enabled parents to have a greater awareness of what their child was experiencing on a surface level. However, no one strategy allowed a depth of understanding as to how their children were learning or how as parents they could support and extend this learning. Neither did the strategy enable us to really learn from parents about their children and use this understanding in developing the work undertaken at the nursery.

As a team we reflected upon the elements of our practice that we wished to develop. We then shared these with a smaller focus group of parents, which gave us the collaborative aims of:

- developing effective dialogue with parents about their child's learning at home and the nursery;
- developing a shared understanding of the theoretical concepts underpinning children's learning;
- developing a shared understanding of how best to support children's learning in both the nursery and the home environment;
- sharing in strategies used in both the home and nursery environments that engage children in their learning;
- determining methods of documenting children's learning that are purposeful to both the home and nursery learning environments.

We wanted to make the revolutionary move forward in developing our pedagogy through recording and dialoguing our shared professional concept with parents of how their children learn (Athey 1990). The challenge now came in developing a framework that would enable this to happen and be sustainable to the needs of the families and nursery.

As a staff team we recognized that the exchange of information with parents was relatively strong, relations were responsive and nurturing and staff sought to support parents in their parenting wherever possible. It was perhaps however an imbalanced approach in terms of competencies of parents and confidence of staff. We needed accessible routes that met the needs of all families and practitioners for the benefit of the children (Whalley 2007). We reflected upon the current effectiveness of our interactions with parents. We questioned how the initial relationships were formed and recognized that, where a home visit had taken place followed by condensed settling sessions, the trust between parent and key person was greater. Time had been invested by both parties to ensure the well-being of the child and this commitment to partnership working from the beginning of the relationship enabled a more open dialogue, in which anxiety and concerns were more readily addressed without fear of judgement.

The development of a shared understanding of the theoretical concepts underpinning children's learning took place through a variety of forms. Documentation of children's learning includes both the Development Matters statements linking to the particular areas of learning and development observed, and also how the child has been learning. Documentation highlights the characteristics of learning observed, and also draws upon supporting theory, for example Laevers' levels of involvement and well-being, or Athey's schematic development.

In addition to this documentation that seeks to make learning visible to parents, information sessions and informal parents groups are delivered by practitioners for parents illustrating the children's learning in situ at the nursery via video vignettes.

Parents are supported to share in their observations of children's learning in the home environment. Patterns of learning displayed both within the home and in the nursery environment are identified and suitably planned for in partnership. Planning sheets were amended, changing the previous guidance points, making suggestions to parents for possible extension activities at home. These planning sheets now include the characteristics of effective learning and what these look like.

Documentation has become a shared process, with digital cameras being used in both the setting and home environments. Images are used to create learning stories for children that offer links between observations of children at play and the Development Matters examples of both what and how children learn.

The impact of a professional learning community at the nursery

The key person approach and mixed age key families

The nursery philosophy is underpinned by a genuine key person approach (Elfer et al. 2003) that values and respects the emotional security and well-being of children, their families and the staff working alongside them.

This approach sees babies and children cared for by one significant adult, who ensures that throughout the busy and active nursery day, each and every child within their care feels known and special. Staff work tirelessly to ensure that the relationships they establish with children are personal and responsive to the individual, enabling children to grow in confidence and independence. Offering a 'professional love' and intimacy (Nutbrown and Page 2008) it is as though the child is 'camped out in the key person's mind' (Elfer et al. 2003: 18). Staff avoid at all costs the conveyor belt of care still seen in some settings.

The high professional energy required to fulfil such a role often fails to gain the appropriate recognition that sees 'the key person approach as intense, hard work, and a big commitment' (Elfer et al. 2003: 18) and it is no wonder that the role of a key person often arises as a discussion topic. The demand upon staff to implement the key person approach effectively and successfully is great. Alongside this all staff recognize the adverse impact ineffective key person relationships can have for children and families and this recognition of the importance of the role brings its own pressure to succeed. At Norland Nursery the role has a further dimension of complexity, in that children are cared for in mixed age key families. Children remain with the same key person for the duration of their time at the nursery, thus avoiding unnecessary transitions between key groups as they move through age and stage related rooms. Indeed the free flow mixed ages enable stability for all members of the nursery with staff and children retaining their room bases adding to the sense of belonging felt within the nursery.

The argument for mixed age grouping is strong and becoming influential, with emotional well-being being linked as a key factor in the development of emotional intelligence (Salovey and Mayer 1990; Goleman 1996). Research supports us in our understanding that caring for and educating children in mixed age key families supports emotional, cognitive and spiritual development. It enables children to develop a sense of themselves, to be social, to be close to others, to recognize their feelings and the feelings of others and to develop relationships. 'Although humans are not usually born in litters, we seem to insist that they be educated in them' (Katz et al. 1990).

Relationships between children

The relationship between children cared for in mixed age groupings also promotes a learning community in its own right, clearly evidenced through the daily interactions of children learning together and from each other.

Transferring our understanding of sibling relationships to the concept of mixed age key families (Dunn and Kendrick 1982) we are able to identify the younger children in our care imitating older or more able peers. This illustrates the theory of peer scaffolding (Vygotsky 1978) as children are observed working cooperatively, practising the skills of negotiation and cooperation as well as developing the emotional intelligence needed to establish sound characteristics for learning.

Observations of young children in contact with each other have highlighted deliberate patterns of social play – mobile babies, for instance, establishing a joint focus of interest through their newly found physical ability. With children around 2½ years old more coordinated play is observed involving imitation. From the age of

3 cooperative play with peer groups develops and becomes the basis for friendships to develop (Goldschmied and Jackson 1994; Bruce 2001). All of these are crucial stages for children to share and we believe that it is preferable for children to work alongside other children of mixed ages and abilities, thus gaining the widest range of interaction possible from which to gain emotional and social awareness and develop their skills in playing and exploring, active learning and creating and thinking critically – the characteristics of early learning.

Partnership working

Our established key family approach also supports a deeper level of partnership working. Maintaining the same key people to work alongside a family offers the opportunity for a depth of relationship between parents and key person leading to a strong and secure relationship.

A genuine key person approach is integral in the implementation of the EYFS (DfE 2012) in which the following key messages are promoted:

- All parents can enhance their children's learning and development.
- Parents have a right to play a central role in making decisions about their child's care and education at every level.
- Successful relationships between parents and educators can have a long lasting and beneficial effect on children's learning and well-being.

Creating an enabling learning environment to provoke and extend children's learning

Over the last two years as the professional learning community has evolved at the nursery there has been a positive shift in the pedagogical confidence of staff. They have moved from delivering a curriculum to planning for learning opportunities that spark and ignite enthusiasm for knowledge and skills among the children, their families and the staff team. One of the aspects of the provision most significantly developed through the learning community is the way in which the learning environment is presented to the children and the ways in which staff use the environment to support and facilitate the learning taking place.

How the environments are used at Norland Nursery

We have five large interconnected indoor learning areas which offer a range of rich continuous provision enhanced daily through observation of individual children's interests, and the learning they are completing through the visits and exploration of their wider community.

Each room is subtly themed through discovery, creation, reflection, technology and the baby nest, all seamlessly interweaving the seven areas of learning, and embracing the characteristics of effective learning.

The garden, our sixth learning space, is accessed from the centre of the building, being open all day as an extension of the free flow practice. The learning community has empowered staff to use the physical resources available to them, thus effectively supporting children to become active, independent, confident and autonomous learners. Observations of children at play are used within team times and alongside parents to explore not just what children are learning but how they are learning, and how best we can extend this, through our own interactions and the enhancement of the learning environment.

The use of provocations as explored within a study tour to the Reggio Emilia Preschools has inspired us to facilitate the children's learning not just within the immediate environment of the nursery but also by weaving some of the richest learning opportunities through our wider community.

Using observations of children's learning as a starting point, in partnership with parents staff share in their understanding of children's interests. Small groups of children who hold similar interests within their learning are determined with opportunities planned for that inspire and challenge children's thoughts, provoking new learning. Via the learning communities staff have reflected upon and documented how the provocations cross boundaries through the children's learning. They have recognized that by embracing a system of planning for provocations they are able to facilitate the children's understanding further, and add further dimensions to their own learning and practice.

Through the reflective conversations held and the open dialogue encouraged as a learning community staff and parents view themselves as co-constructors of knowledge as they work alongside each other and the children in areas where resources have been carefully selected to offer open-ended learning opportunities, where children's creativity can flow and critical thinking develop. Here are two parents talking about their experience.

I've loved being able to share in Lily's learning with her key person. It's been great to understand why she is doing the things she does and what I can do at home to support her. We now share everything about Lily and I feel that I am able to offer her so much more that really means something to her.

The nursery has been brilliant at establishing a real community feel, everyone in the family is included and valued. I know and understand so much about my boys, what they are doing, how they are learning. Everything that we do at home and the things we share with nursery are always used to the boys' benefit. The time and energy that is placed into really getting to know us and then to work with us is amazing.

At the nursery children are recognized as 'active social agents' and 'meaning makers' and consequently the nursery is free flow and workshop based. Spaces have been designed that enable children to make meaningful exchanges, to review their learning and extend their understanding of what they have shared within the wider community. Each of the rooms brings rich experiences in its own right, outdoors we grow and harvest our own vegetables, and make use of our nursery created mini play pod and a stage where children are free to explore their theatrical talents, such as our recent production of *The Tempest* following a nursery visit to the Globe Theatre in London.

A large indoor beach with guttering and a pulley system joins the water space, enabling children to make the cement needed to hold together the constructions previously designed in the technology room following their visit to the building sites. Children are seen to display deep-level learning as they work through early science and maths, negotiating and forming hypotheses together.

Children are supported to engage with real tools. For example, the woodwork bench facilitates the hammering of nails, and even the investigation of car parts following a visit by the children to the local garage and car wash after they became interested in vehicles, having watched the refitting of a new windscreen to a staff member's car in the playground.

A resident artist supports the creative child in expressing their thoughts. Working within the Atelier (our creative area), staff engage in the development of large scale projects created with recyclable, natural, non-commercial and commercial materials to extend children's creativity.

Emotionally secure spaces are available for children to move from and return to, with each key family having a base room acting as their 'island of intimacy' in which children are able to share with their key person and key family, offering children a sense of belonging. Nests allow babies and younger children the space to disengage and rest, thus enhancing levels of physical and emotional well-being.

The benefits of the work undertaken at the nursery are vast, with children displaying high levels of well-being and involvement (Laevers 1997). Children's progression is carefully monitored and we are confident all children will meet their full potential within our care, with many exceeding expectations. The free flow environment is enabling children to become autonomous in their learning, making choices and taking suitable risk. The mixed age grouping allows older children to show care and responsibility to those younger than themselves, role modelling skills such as negotiation, cooperation and turn taking.

We are still on our journey but when we look at the learning taking place between children, parents and staff explored throughout this chapter it seems that creating and embracing a professional learning community has enabled, empowered and deepened the learning of stakeholders. Children, parents and staff celebrate how they learn as well as what they learn. Children and adults have been encouraged to be active learners, playing and exploring and thinking critically as they develop skill, will and thrill as individuals and as members of Norland's unique learning community.

References

Athey, C. (1990) *Extending Thought in Young Children: A Parent-Teacher Partnership.* London: Paul Chapman Publishing.

Athey, C. (2004) Pedagogical Leadership *in Pedagogical Leadership.* Nottingham: NCSL.

Bell, J. (2005) *Doing your Research Project.* Maidenhead: McGraw-Hill.

Bruce, T. (2001) *Learning Through Play: Babies, Toddlers and the Foundation Years.* London: Hodder and Stoughton.

Crowther, C. (2012a) EYFS best practice: prime time – under threes . . . Physical Development, *Nursery World*, July 9.

Crowther, C. (2012b) EYFS best practice: prime time – under threes . . . Personal, Social and Emotional Development, *Nursery World*, August 6.

Crowther, C. (2012c) EYFS best practice: prime time – under threes . . . Communication and Language, *Nursery World*, September 3.

DfE (Department for Education) (2012) *Statutory Framework for the Early Years Foundation Stage: Setting the Standards for Learning, Development and Care for Children from Birth to Five.* http://www.foundationyears.org.uk/early-years-foundation-stage-2012/ or http://www.education.gov.uk/aboutdfe/statutory/g00213120/eyfs-statutory-framework (accessed 1 January 2013).

Dunn, J. and Kendrick, P. (1982) *The Beginnings of Social Understanding.* Oxford: Blackwell.

Elfer, P., Goldschmied, E. and Selleck, D. (2003) *Key Persons in the Nursery: Building Relationships for Quality Provision.* London: David Fulton Publishers.

Goldschmied, E. and Jackson, S. (1994) *People Under Three: Young Children in Daycare.* London: Routledge.

Goleman, D. (1996) *Emotional Intelligence.* London: Bloomsbury.

Hasenfield, Y. (1983) *Human Service Organizations.* Engelwood Cliffs, NJ: Prentice Hall.

Jorde-Bloom, P. (1992) *Avoiding Burnout: Strategies for Managing Time, Space and People in Early Childhood Education.* Mt Rainier, Washington, DC: Grypton House.

Katz, L.G., Evangelou, D. and Hartman, J.A. (1990) *The Case for Mixed-age Grouping in Early Education.* Washington, DC: National Association for the Education of Young Children.

Kolb, D.A. with Osland, J. and Rubin, I. (1995) *Organizational Behavior: An Experiential Approach to Human Behavior in Organizations.* Englewood Cliffs, NJ: Prentice Hall.

Laevers, F. (1997) *A Process-oriented Child Follow-up System for Young Children.* Leuven, Belgium: Centre for Experiential Education.

Law, S. and Glover, D. (2000) *Educational Leadership and Learning: Practice, Policy and Research.* Buckingham: Open University Press.

Malaguzzi, L. (1993) History, ideas, and basic philosophy, in C. Edwards, L. Gandini and G. Forman (eds) *The Hundred Languages of Children: The Reggio Emilia Approach to Early Childhood Education*. Norwood, NJ: Ablex Publishing.

Marshall, J. (1994) Revisioning organisations by developing female values, in J. Boot, J. Lawrence and J. Morris (eds) *Managing the Unknown by Creating New Futures*. London: McGraw-Hill.

Midgley, C. and Wood, S. (1993) Beyond site-based management: empowering teachers to reform schools, *Phi Delta Kappan*, 75(3): 245–52.

Nutbrown, C. (2012) *Foundations for Quality. The Independent Review of Early Education and Childcare Qualification, Final Report*. Runcorn: Department for Education.

Nutbrown, C. and Page, J. (2008) *Working with Babies and Children from Birth to Three*. London: Sage.

Robbins, A. (2001) *Awaken the Giant Within*. London: Simon and Schuster.

Rodd, J. (2010) *Leadership in Early Childhood*, 3rd edn. Maidenhead: Open University Press.

Salovey, P. and Mayer, J. (1990) Emotional intelligence, *Imagination, Cognition and Personality*, 9: 185–211.

Sylva, K., Melhuish, E., Sammons, P., Siraj-Blatchford, I. and Taggart, B. (2004) *The Effective Provision of Pre-school Education*. London: DfES Publications.

Vander Ven, K. (1988) Pathways to professional effectiveness in early childhood educators, in B. Spodek, O. Saracho and D. Peters (eds) *Professionalism and the Early Childhood Practitioner*. New York: Teachers College Press.

Vygotsky, L.S. (1978) *Mind in Society: The Development of Higher Psychological Processes*. Cambridge, MA: Harvard College.

Whalley, M. (2006) Leadership in integrated centres and services for children and families – a community development approach: engaging with the struggle, *Children Issues*, 10(2): 8.

Whalley, M. (2007) *Involving Parents in their Children's Learning*, 2nd edn. London: Paul Chapman Publishing.

Whalley, M. (2011) Personal conference notes.

8 Improving the learning in primary schools: building on the early years

Kim Porter

The aim of this book is to help practitioners understand more about how children learn and to reflect on the implications of that understanding for working in the early years. In this final chapter we look beyond the EYFS into Key Stage 1. What are the implications for practitioners of what we know about how children learn and what impact and relevance do the Characteristics of Effective Learning have beyond the end of the reception year? Is there still a place for play and exploration in Key Stage 1? What would active learning in primary school look like? How can practitioners provide opportunities for creating and thinking critically in Year 1 and beyond?

Despite the fact that many of the values central to the EYFS are also core to post 16 learning, with independence, critical thought and self-reliance strong elements of both further and higher education, something altogether different shapes the experiences of pupils in the vast majority of our primary and secondary schools.

The constant drive towards a raising of standards within a narrow field fundamentally shifts practice in our classrooms. Measuring achievement only in certain subjects changes our prioritization. Martin Roth, director of the Victoria and Albert Museum, has warned that we are in danger of destroying Britain's creative economy 'within a generation' if the arts based subjects are pushed out of the curriculum. Meanwhile the Confederation of British Industry (CBI) has been equally active in criticizing the current 'conveyor belt approach' to education and calling for a 'new performance standard based on the whole person we want to develop and a rigorous and demanding accountability regime that assesses schools' performance on a wider basis than the narrow measure of exams' (CBI 2012).

A brief look back through recent educational history reminds us of the continuing search for better ways to raise standards of educational achievement. Successive governments have introduced piecemeal education reforms since the mid-1970s designed to improve performance in the UK, but because they have only been partial in their aims, they have been partial in their success. The results have been steady movements in the right direction rather than seismic shifts, judged by both our own and international benchmarks.

Since former Prime Minister Jim Callaghan's groundbreaking Ruskin College speech of 1976, which is widely regarded as having begun 'The Great Debate' about the nature and purpose of public education, governments of all parties have accepted that education should seek to improve outcomes and prospects for all children. However, Callaghan's criticism that the education system in the mid-1970s was 'fitting a so-called inferior group of children with just enough learning to earn their living in the factory' (Callaghan 1976) has continuing resonance today. Despite (or perhaps because of) all of the reforms and changes including the National Curriculum, targets, testing, the 'creative' curriculum, as well as a current government agenda which leans towards times tables, Latin, Greek and grammar, the overall experience of pupils in primary schools remains firmly about *what* they learn not *how* they learn, and risks fitting them with nothing more than an updated modernized version of 'just enough learning'.

The Plowden Report was published a long time ago but set a different and alternative tone and continues to challenge successive governments' top down initiatives: 'At the heart of the educational process lies the child. No advances in policy, no acquisitions of new equipment, have their desired effect unless they are in harmony with the child' (CACE 1967).

Simultaneously with the top down curriculum and target driven approach which has been pursued by successive governments, there have been other strong voices, demanding the recognition of the child's development and perspective, and schools full of initiatives. These are designed to raise the child's profile – Student Councils, Investors in Pupils, Pupil Voice – as well as strong efforts to support social and personal development, social and emotional aspects of learning (SEAL; DCSF 2005), for example. Practitioners in primary schools have been remarkably resilient to changes that have often made little sense to them in terms of classroom practice. Keeping a firm grip on child development and pedagogy is a constant challenge and is sometimes portrayed as oppositional to government reforms.

Could it be that the most recent changes to the Ofsted framework (Ofsted 2012a) in combination with the revised EYFS emphasis on effective learning characteristics and alongside strong voices of discontent from outside the educational sector, allow us an opportunity to change our practices in school in a way previously difficult for all except the very brave?

This chapter explores this notion further. How does the current Ofsted framework support a characteristics driven model? Does the revised EYFS Statutory Framework (DfE 2012) provide an opportunity to change Key Stage 1 practice or make its formality a bygone conclusion, with statements on 'school readiness' already challenging schools? What does the research in England and elsewhere tell us? What are the barriers that prevent practitioners from adopting a philosophy where engagement, motivation and thinking are central to planning and provision and how can these be overcome? Two contemporary case studies along with practical suggestions will suggest ways for practitioners to respond proactively and differently to the drive towards 'more formal learning' in Year 1.

Painting the picture: Key Stage 1 in 2013

Let's return to the whiteboard-face and take a snapshot of current Year 1 and Year 2 provision and practice. In recent years two key trends have been shaping the land-scape of teaching in Key Stage 1: a continued drive to raise standards at the end of Year 2, in combination with an increasing acknowledgement that many children leave the EYFS without the necessary maturity to begin a more formal and subject specific curriculum.

Transition between reception year and Year 1 has become central to school conversations – acknowledging the gulf between two curriculums that challenge all but the most resilient of our children. This has led schools in two very different directions, often dependent on the philosophy of leadership and the reality of the school's situation.

Some schools have pushed what they perceive to be a 'school readiness' agenda into an increased formalization in the final term of the reception year. This usually involves more time on the carpet or at tables and a greater emphasis on adult-led activities, to enable children to 'hit the ground running' when they enter Year 1. Playful and play-based learning is reduced.

In other schools, the first term of Year 1 has become the key transition point. Classrooms have been reorganized to include some continuous provision and children are encouraged to use these at certain times. All too often in these schools an uneasy and well-intended compromise is reached whereby a nod is given to the importance of the continuation of EYFS pedagogy. Environments look familiar to children and 'playing' is allowed at certain times, generally after 'work' has been finished or during 'golden time' or the equivalent – which may be very time restricted. It is rare to see the areas of continuous provision being used as a base for teaching activities.

In an ironic twist the higher attaining children who do finish 'work' are most likely to access the areas, even though the provision has been placed in class with lower attainers in mind. Continuous provision is rarer still in Year 2 classes, although 'small world', 'construction' and reading areas are sometimes seen where there is space in schools. Sometimes a shared area outside the classroom is set up to offer this provision, for example a themed role play area, which is shared by year groups and classes.

In addition to physical changes to Key Stage 1 classrooms, many primary schools have explored the concept of different learning styles and have adapted some aspects of teaching accordingly. Good teachers know that they need to offer a range of styles which appeal to visual, auditory and kinaesthetic learners (VAK or VARK model) and plan their lessons with these in mind. Teachers leave initial training understanding the importance of learning styles and Ofsted have been keen to link this to good practice around personalized learning.

Dunn and Dunn (1978), for example, have taken Neil Fleming's VAK/VARK model and have argued that teachers should try to make changes in their classrooms that will be beneficial to every learning style. Despite voices of concern about school's simplification of the VAK/VARK models, even those like Professor Guy Claxton (2009) who are doubtful of the scientific evidence, accept that it is helpful for teachers to be thinking more about how learners learn. Multi-sensory opportunities have increased; more effective use is made of puppets and resources for example; some teachers have successfully found ways of engaging their pupils in what is still fundamentally a transmission oriented culture.

School readiness versus life readiness

> Children's readiness for school affects their learning and development. Schools' readiness for children ensures learning environments are child-friendly and adapt to the diverse needs of young learners and their families.
> (UNICEF 2008)

Year 1 and Year 2 practitioners frequently talk of the tension between the demands of curriculum coverage in a results driven system which leads their daily practice to be at odds with what they may fundamentally believe about how young children learn. Practitioners talk of being stuck between the proverbial rock and a hard place; they may value the early years pedagogy but they are worried that their children will not make sufficient progress due to a lack of formalized teaching.

Opposition from senior leaders and increased parental demands are also cited as reasons Year 1 and Year 2 teachers conform to a teaching system which requires an about face from previous pedagogy. Practitioners new to Key Stage 1 will mostly perpetuate the provision that they see on initial training or as newly qualified teachers, thereby continuing the same culture of expectation in their own practice.

Some Key Stage 1 practitioners can be critical of the EYFS curriculum and staff for a lack of what is perceived as appropriate preparation for school readiness. The recent introduction of the statutory phonics screening check in June of Year 1 is a further source of tension. The lack of definition of 'school readiness' in the EYFS Statutory Framework has led to a broad church of interpretation at setting and school level, with everything from toileting, to handwriting, to language, to behaviour on the agenda.

Whitebread and Bingham (2012) provide critical research evidence that children are always ready to learn rather than necessarily being ready for school. The focus, they argue, should be about life preparation rather than school preparation, and they are entirely in tune in this respect with the CBI who think education should be about 'developing a pattern of behaviour, thinking and feeling based on sound principles, integrity and resilience' which 'involves broadening our traditional expectation . . . to help bring out those qualities in young people' (CBI 2012).

As one Year 2 pupil recently observed in conversation over school dinner, 'when we grow up we don't live in schools', acknowledging the gulf between what happens in school and what happens beyond the school gates.

The importance of effective transition

As we have discussed, with two very different curriculums smooth transition becomes of fundamental importance. Ideally children would move into Year 1 with their enthusiasm for learning intact and progress would ensue without the regression so often seen. Certainly the systems in place do not help, especially those around assessment.

The continuing search for a straight line of progress and attainment from the end of reception to the end of Key Stage 1 (then to the end of Key Stage 2 and onwards to GCSE grades) has spawned a veritable industry of tracking systems. Teachers in Year 1 have to move children from the EYFS assessment system to national curriculum levels, and again this happens at various points according to school protocols. The changes to summative assessment in the revised EYFS are unlikely to make this transfer of information any easier. Best fit judgements of children at the end of reception as emerging (working towards), expected (working within) or exceeding (working beyond) the ELGs are likely to provide Year 1 teachers with as many questions as answers.

Common sense tells teachers that those already achieving well at the end of EYFS should go on to achieve well throughout their school career. However, to paraphrase Barry Hymer at the North of England Conference 2012, 'no one knows his or her own potential let alone anyone else's . . . potential is different from ability'.

Although the gap between vulnerable groups and the median in good levels of development is slowly narrowing (EYFSP data trends 2010–2012), there remains a significant gap between summer-born children and their peers. There is a danger that these children can be labelled as lower attainers with a trajectory assumed accordingly, despite evidence that maturity rather than ability is the issue.

Despite continuing issues with summative assessment systems, there is much anecdotal evidence from teachers and headteachers to suggest that transition is much improved in many schools. Schools acknowledge that transition is something worth spending some time and resource on. Effective transition happens when schools focus on keeping what they can the same and preparing children (and their parents) for that which will change. In some schools the process is more than a one-off event, and genuinely involves the children at the core. However, even when it is highly valued, good practice in transition is, in the main, focused on environments and a notional concept of play-based learning.

In the best examples, practitioners who are trained in early years are able to take that philosophy into a Year 1 classroom. However, in many cases, Year 1 practitioners try to do the equivalent of a teaching and learning 'pick and mix,' trying to blend the two curriculums, but always with the focus being on *what* the children are learning. Those who can commit to taking the characteristics of effective learning into Key Stage 1, to focus on how children are learning, and furthermore understand how that changes their traditional teacher role, will be advantaged greatly in the transition process – as will the children and families with whom they work.

How theory and research can support the characteristics in Key Stage 1

Early years research is rich in examples of the efficacy of supporting practitioners' understanding of how young children learn. Constructing children as actively contributing to and shaping their own learning, and acquiring knowledge through interactions with adults and peers, is characteristic of much of early years pedagogy. This includes eminent work from Isaacs (1932) through to the Effective Provision of Preschool Education (EPPE) study and the associated investigation of effective pedagogy (Siraj-Blatchford and Sylva 2004).

There is a continuing danger of seeing this research in isolation from how older children learn, although many commentators and researchers have evidence to suggest that, not surprisingly, children and adults do learn best when they are motivated, engaged and thinking critically.

There is considerable research from the United Kingdom and further afield that supports the positive impact of taking active learning, play, exploration and creating and thinking critically beyond the EYFS. Margaret Donaldson's seminal *Children's Minds* (1978) posed and attempted to answer the crucial question of 'What makes us want to learn?' It is in the answer to this query that we plan lessons, environments, classrooms and schools that excite and motivate the young children with whom we work. Donaldson concluded that humans have a fundamental urge to 'be effective, competent and independent, to understand the world and to act with skill'. Practitioners who can provide tasks that are intrinsically motivating, with just the right balance of success and challenge, avoid having to resort to one of the many reward systems which operate in our schools. Building on children's natural thirst for skill and knowledge which links to their own interests is central to early years principles, yet often absent in Year 1 and beyond, so external motivation becomes necessary: stickers, certificates and credits become core to everyday classroom practice.

Children are motivated to behave through traffic light systems, keeping 'on the sun not in the cloud', being 'good to be green'. Behaviours that were not an issue in EYFS can easily become so in Year 1 with children being asked to switch from a curriculum with them at the heart to one with the National Curriculum at the centre.

The Rose Report (DCSF 2009) and the Cambridge Primary Review (Alexander 2009) have both suggested that active, interactive and collaborative learning experiences would be of benefit beyond the pre-school years, arguing that the educational experiences that children have as they begin primary school should capitalize on their natural appetite for learning and practical activities and encourage early confidence and enthusiasm. The change of UK government in 2010 altered the direction in which schools had started to move; many had already embraced a more creative curriculum where speaking and listening were reinvigorated.

Scandinavian and central European countries have long traditions of education systems based on a social constructivist model, and these countries have been visited frequently in recent years by teachers and educational professional searching for concrete evidence of an alternative way of working. The Reggio Emilia Approach to early years education is frequently cited and adapted for use by practitioners in the UK (see, for example, Chapters 5 and 7 in this book).

Recent research supports this approach if we take a long term view. For example, in a recent study of children's reading, there was no significant difference in reading at age 11 for those children that had begun early or at 7. Those who began early made a better start and were further ahead by 7, however they were on a par by age 11 and were quicker to lose motivation and interest in their mid-teens (Suggate 2007).

A newspaper article in *The Guardian* (Kingsley 2012) on the Lumiar schools, founded by businessman Ricardo Semler in 2003, asked whether formal teaching in its conventional sense could ever breed creativity, and concluded that it could not. Semler believed that children learn best when they have a say in what they are learning and it was on this principle that Lumiar's project-based system was founded.

> Lumiar's progressive teachers don't teach from a syllabus. In fact, they're not even called teachers. They're called mentors, and what they teach their charges (aged 0–14) is mainly agreed through discussion with the children themselves. They have no lessons in the traditional sense, nor homework. Instead, the children work on 'projects', either suggested by their mentors, or invented by the pupils.
>
> (Kingsley 2012)

Lumiar philosophy is that learning is not synonymous with absorbing and accumulating information. Learning is becoming capable of doing something you could not do previously. 'This vision of learning implies that learning is something eminently active (interactive, collaborative), related above all to things one becomes capable of doing' (see http://lumiarschool.wordpress.com/). The radical approach has many enthusiasts, with a recent survey conducted by UNESCO, Stanford University and Microsoft naming Lumiar as one of the 12 most innovative schools in the world.

Nearer to England, Northern Ireland, in line with many other countries, has acknowledged the need for a curriculum which shows a decreased emphasis on content knowledge and increased emphasis on transferable skills such as critical and creative thinking. The early years are seen to reach beyond the age of 5. The Northern Ireland Council for Curriculum, Examinations and Assessment (CCEA) states that 'children learn best when learning is interactive, practical and enjoyable for both children and teachers' (CCEA 2007). 'Thinking skills and personal capabilities' are an integral feature of the Year 1 and Year 2 Foundation Stage Curriculum (CCEA 2007). In Wales the Foundation Stage recommends a focus on 'play/active learning' and 'active educational play' for children aged from 3 to 7 years old (Welsh Assembly Government 2008).

In Scotland a restructuring of the National Curriculum has created an Early Level which encompasses the two years of part-time preschool education available to all children along with the first year of primary school (Learning and Teaching Scotland 2009). The practice guidance for this Early Level directs teachers responsible for the first class in primary school to adopt an 'active learning' pedagogy.

Theory and research provide plentiful evidence that would support the continuation of the characteristics approach beyond reception, and remind us that in many ways, England is out of sync with the rest of the United Kingdom as regards its current primary philosophy.

The research also suggests that if schools move to a model which takes early years principles into primary school, they need to do so in full understanding of the different role of the teacher. Action research carried out by a team in Scotland found gaps between practitioners' commitment to active learning and the reality of daily practice. Their paper charts researchers who followed five teachers in four primary schools over the course of a year, working in schools where there was a commitment to active learning, and concluded that 'the evidence we gathered suggested that while there have been innovations in practice, these may perhaps best be described as changes in degree rather than revolutionary departures' (Stephen et al. 2009). Although the researchers saw many examples of planned purposeful play and of alternative resources to pen and paper being used, they did not see anything they could describe as spontaneous play. The observed activities did not arise from the children's everyday experiences, and the researchers felt that teachers' training did not engage them with thinking about their role as a teacher.

How the revised Ofsted inspection framework can support the characteristics in Key Stage 1

In September 2012, the third change in just over a year was made to the inspection framework for schools in England. The changes made to the framework are significant, and present increased possibilities for creative and innovative practice in Key Stage 1 classrooms. At the heart of this change lies a seeming contradiction between

Ofsted and the Department of Education's drive to formalized teaching with the new Ofsted inspection framework fundamentally being about children's learning and how this can best be achieved (Ofsted 2012a).

Inspectors have been directed to leave their own subjective views on styles of teaching at the door and observe the learning in lessons. What are pupils doing? Are they all actively engaged? Do children know what they need to do to improve? This is a genuine opportunity for practitioners to organize their environment, resources and delivery in a non-traditional way, and for children who are motivated, engaged, persistent and thoughtful to show the progress they are making.

The most important change is the movement from judgement on teaching to a judgement on learning. There are no prescribed methodologies so the structure of the lesson is no longer relevant and the teacher as transmitter is not the desired status quo. The Ofsted criterion for effective teaching for any age group is that it secures engagement, interest and concentration, determination, resilience and independence. The focus is on the children, what they are learning, and the progress they are making. Children need to be able to discuss and describe their learning, and practitioners who keep the characteristics central to planning and provision will be rewarded with pupils who are able to work independently, to think about their learning and to articulate that learning.

Ofsted's own good practice guides celebrate such learning throughout primary years, for example *An Enquiry-based Approach to Learning* (Ofsted 2012b) which follows a Year 6 class and *Preparing Children to be 21st Century Citizens, Contributing to Sustainable Communities* (Ofsted 2012c). The current inspection regime supports practitioners to develop a 'how you learn' in addition to 'what you learn' approach as it values key characteristics of learning skills.

Best practice and case studies

Case Study 1: Year 1, Horsforth Newlaithes Primary School, Leeds

Newlaithes was a junior school until September 2011 when it took in an intake of 60 reception children in a new building attached to the old site. Elizabeth Deare was employed as Foundation Leader and tasked with setting up the new unit. Inspired by a visit to Reggio Emilia two years earlier, she saw this as an opportunity to implement an educational philosophy that could draw on the work of Sir Ken Robinson (1999) and child development theory and practice.

The first year was very successful with 82 per cent of the children achieving a good level of development (GLD), making good progress from entry points. Parents, key partners from the beginning, were delighted with the skills their children had developed: children were exhibiting strong well-being and had effective 'learning to learn' skills. Parents wanted to see a continuation of the provision, and Elizabeth was able to build on this as they planned for the children's move into Year 1.

The staff were always very clear on their philosophy of education and adopted some non-negotiables which set the path for the provision. 'We were certain that children, as active protagonists in their own learning, had to have control . . . We knew that to make learning fun it had to be relevant and hands on with a great deal of play. We knew that the Personal Social and Emotional Development (PSED) levels were of the utmost importance and that we owed the children to provide them with life skills. They deserved to be independent risk takers who weren't afraid to be wrong and who persevered, children who could manage their own time and conduct their own research and learning . . . they needed to be collaborative and learn to negotiate, speak well and listen constructively. Finally, we knew involving parents and the wider family was important as we are all responsible for the children's learning.'

The Year 1 area was divided into four learning spaces which the 60 children can move across – with a huge variety of areas of provision including a large outdoor area with a small wood. At the start of the year the children developed two imaginary communities – Beech Forest and Magical Forest. These communities belong to the children and are used as hangers for the curriculum work.

Within these communities the children have developed their own characters with homes and jobs. Through these invented places the children have been involved in drama, literacy, maths, science, design technology, geography, dance and art work, as well as opportunities for problem-solving and discussing philosophical and ethical dilemmas. Using these places as a starting point has meant the children are intrinsically motivated and in control of the direction of their learning.

The children's search for a thief in the community led them to look for clues around the setting. They made a huge footprint pictogram in order to eliminate Year 1 children from the enquiries. The pupils have talked to a police officer, a barrister and a politics lecturer to develop the communities' justice systems. There are two constitutions written by the children and there has been a state opening of the Forest Parliament to declare the communities open. After one child said that thieves were 'not all bad but just very poor' an active discussion considered this idea and looked at how our communities care for disadvantaged people.

The children work on small group projects which they run without an adult most of the time, a progression from reception where the children worked on small group projects with an adult. The children meet with an adult at the start of the week to decide on the nature and direction of the project and then in their own time they conduct the work as a group. This has been very successful for developing personal, social and emotional skills; speaking and listening skills; and life skills. There has been huge progress in the children's development in these areas and this is impacting on all learning including reading, writing and maths.

With purpose and enjoyment at the core, the staff teach reading and writing through the community work but they also have Reading and Writing Workshops. In Reading Workshop the children choose a book nook which is a cosy place in the Piazza, the central space, and read alone or with friends, or with the house rabbit.

At the recent parents' consultation evening a significant number of parents commented on their children's positive attitude to reading which they see as both enjoyable and relaxing. In Writing Workshop the children choose what they write about and teachers develop next steps but through their chosen focus. Pupils are motivated to write as they have more ownership and control. Genres and text types are taught through daily literacy sessions. There are also daily maths and phonics sessions.

The concern for the school has been ensuring curriculum coverage while using this approach. So far it is going well, with recent levelling of reading, writing and maths showing a significant majority of children working at 1b to 2b in all three areas and pupils progressing well in all areas.

'It has been, and will continue to be, a challenge for us to hold onto the things we know are important as the curriculum is tight and getting even more prescriptive and knowledge based rather than skills led which it needs to be in these ever changing times.' (Quoted material from Elizabeth Deare, Horsforth Newthlaites Primary School)

Case Study 2: Partnership of Tinderwood Trust and Central Street Infant School – the impact of Forest School on Key Stage 1 children

Emily Jones, Project Developer and Forest School Leader for Tinderwood Trust, describes the impact on two Key Stage 1 boys of the Forest School approach, which encompasses all aspects of the effective learning characteristics.

Jack is in Key Stage 1 of a small Infants school. He is a creative, physical child with bucketloads of potential but hardly anywhere at all to put it. He is quiet, thoughtful and frustrated and to his teachers he presents as shy and a little mischievous.

Jack has been going to Forest School as part of a weekly project run by Tinderwood in school time. (Parental requests for Forest School opportunities for their children led to the school approaching Tinderwood to work with them. The project was partly funded by National Lottery money, allocated to Tinderwood Trust to work with several schools in the Upper Calder Valley area.)

At Forest School Jack has a really good friend who he trusts. His friend is quiet; his friend never says anything in school and doesn't really like school. His mum is worried that he never talks about what he has been learning or doing. His name is Billy. The session described below took place six or seven weeks into the project.

From the stash of possible resources to use at today's Forest School session, in the beautiful woods which they have begun to love, Jack and Billy have chosen a rope. One rope. It is blue and quite long. No one has asked them to take the rope but they know that all the resources are there to be cared for and used as and when needed. They know the good spots in the woods now and they know how far they can go before they are out of the Forest School site; the flag markers tell them that.

At this Forest School site there is a ditch, quite deep and wide with a little trickle of a stream at the bottom of it. This is Jack and Billy's favourite spot. Others prefer over near where they found the animal skeleton, or up where the big rocks are covered in moss, or further over the site where the big beech trees hold out good big branches to make the swing in the tree fly far up and out over the bluebells and ferns down below. But Jack and Billy like the ditch.

The Forest School leaders know where Jack and Billy and all the other children are. They have trust and confidence in all the children's abilities now and the staff from school are getting to be more relaxed about the environment in which the children are learning. On one occasion a Forest School leader goes over to the ditch where Jack and Billy are busy. The boys are so deep in their play that they are startled when she speaks to ask if they need anything else fetching. No thank you. Maybe a drink of water and something to eat would be good, she suggests and then leaves them to it. Later she sees them go to the place where the snacks are, wash their hands, grab a quick drink and an apple and then head off back to their own world.

As the session ends, the whole class, adults and children, get together by the fire to share tales of what they have been doing. Every week hands shoot up to tell of adventures and stories, but never Jack or Billy's. So the morning has been busy with all kinds of things going on, shares the Forest School leader. 'I have been busy watching a really beautiful bug with Dan and Will and then they decided to make it an obstacle course didn't you?', she tells as Dan and Will nod proudly. Jack and Billy look fit to burst. Their eyes sparkle with enthusiasm but they have been told so often that they never speak up in class that they have begun to believe it. The Forest School leader knows this.

'So – this piece of blue rope has had a very busy morning', she tells the group, 'Who would like to tell its story?' Jack and Billy's hands are in the air before the words are out of her mouth and they are off.

'That's our special secret communication rope and if you pull it like this it means help and then you have to tie it to a tree and go down the steep edge really carefully because it is slippery, and then when you get there you pull it like this, (and he unties it and brings the end down), and sometimes the emergency is so big that just for a second or two we have to, (he looks around suddenly a bit nervous before he catches the Forest School leader's smile again), sometimes we have to take off our high vis vests and wave them to say okay, okay here I am and then we put them on again really fast.'

They breathe out after this joint stream of words and look so pleased with themselves they are practically glowing. The teachers are stunned.

Jack and Billy rarely have access to learning through play now that they are in Key Stage 1, but they have not finished learning in that way. They are thoughtful, engaged and motivated to learn in the Forest School environment in ways which are just not possible in their normal classroom setting or the school playground. They are active in their own learning; they explore and play games of their own choosing, risking failure by trying out their own ideas, and feeling success from their own endeavours. They have the chance to try out their ideas and build on the challenges they are faced with.

Billy's mum has heard all about Forest School and on those days he is ready for school before she is. Billy has taken his family to the Forest School site and shown them everything and his mum cannot believe his enthusiasm. Jack now knows of different ways to get around challenges, he is less frustrated with classroom life, and sometimes speaks up knowing that the teacher has a different view of him as inventive, able and capable and he is beginning to believe that anything is possible. Success breeds success in the woods.

Practical solutions: how to take the characteristics into Year 1 and Year 2

Although many practitioners may be inspired by these case studies, as well as their reflections on research and their current context to transform their approach, some may wish to begin with a less radical approach to ensuring that engagement, motivation and thinking are key elements to their practice. The following are accessible to all Key Stage 1 practitioners.

Playing and exploring – Engagement
- Finding out and exploring
- Playing with what they know
- Being willing to 'have a go'

Ideas for Key stage 1
- Continue to play with children, to be sensitive and encouraging and give time to feedback (Sutton Trust 2011).
- Provide stimulating and relevant resources, ensure the environment is flexible and not entirely taken with tables and chairs. Ask to sometimes share the outdoor space used by the EYFS children if you have none of your own to use.
- Plan activities which support concentration and remember the value of first-hand experiences.
- Opportunities for role play are plentiful in Key Stage 1, linked to texts and to topics.

- Plan for speaking and listening activities which link into role play and allow children to explore feelings and thought such as hot seating, conscience alley and mantel of the expert.
- Link the science curriculum to being willing to have a go, for example experimentation with forces.
- It is hard to achieve uninterrupted time but it may be possible to do projects which run across sessions and days and allow for pupils to follow particular interests, for example the classic Year 1 'toys' topic could be planned in this way with children engaged with an aspect that they find interesting and want to investigate further.

Active learning – Motivation
- Being involved and concentrating
- Keeping on trying
- Enjoying achieving what they set out to do

Ideas for Key Stage 1
- Continue to support the choice process and to stimulate pupils' interests by providing new and unusual experiences and resources, noticing what arouses their curiosity.
- Plan ahead to meet goals (targets!) with discussion linked to next steps and with specific praise. Encourage a climate where all are learning together and from each other. Spend time talking about learning and explore methods with children such as 'The Pit', which allow them to see that they often learn best when stuck and find a way to move on (Nottingham 2010).
- Read and tell stories to children of those who have bounced back, encouraging them to see the benefit of persistence. Encourage children to have the 'Tigger factor' rather than dreaming they might have the 'X factor'.
- Create an ethos in class based on Barry Hymer's (2012) delightful 'bouncebackability' where effort, patience, small steps and delayed gratification are the order of the day.
- Use stimuli that encourage careful observation and observation of the detail.

Creating and thinking critically – Thinking
- Having their own ideas
- Making links
- Choosing ways to do things

Ideas for Key Stage 1

- Use the language of thinking and learning, encourage open-ended thinking, respect efforts and ideas.
- Model self-talk; give time and value to sustained shared thinking; give time to feedback; model the plan, do, review process.
- Plan activities which give children an opportunity to find their own ways to develop and represent ideas.
- Give opportunities to explore and manipulate materials before a specific 'learning' activity. Evidence from schools where children have been able to play with Numicon resources (hold, stick in play-doh, paint with, use in role play) in every area at a very early age, for example, shows those children are more ready to engage with learning activities. (Numicon is a practical quality first teaching approach designed to give children the understanding of number ideas and number relationships.)
- Provide rich play opportunities, which build on children's experiences in EYFS and extend their learning.
- Use mind mapping when suitable; plan themes and projects together; model your own thinking and encourage apparent non-sequiturs which stimulate thinking and creativity.
- Start topics and themes with a list of children's queries and questions which the learning community will then find out about.
- Encourage staff to ask questions, so that children are reminded that we are all learners.
- Give scope for activities which allow children to plan, do and review, and to talk about their learning. Support this with peer talk, the box Philosophy for Children (P4C) approach or Investors in Pupils.

Conclusions

The purpose of this chapter has been to support primary schools to create a climate in which active learning is promoted and children are authentically engaged. We have seen that Key Stage 1 practitioners are often unwilling participants in a primary education system which shifts uneasily from the preceding EYFS curriculum. Despite theory, research and a general feeling of discontent with the long term impact of a formal and test-based system, schools have generally abandoned what they know about how children learn, and adopted a transmission-based 'empty vessel' approach. This approach has good intentions at its core – how can we improve outcomes for our children? Yet it is seems to be the wrong answer to the right question.

In order to support pupils appropriately practitioners need to be aware that when young children are encouraged to follow their natural instincts to play and explore, allowed to concentrate on self-chosen challenges and supported to plan and review their own learning, they become self-regulated learners who are more likely to achieve socially and academically than children who have been more passive in their learning. They are more likely to access the higher order thinking skills which will allow them to move beyond age-related expectations and to respond creatively yet persistently.

The case studies show that we can operate differently, that we do not need to base our practice on an irrational denial of the importance of the characteristics of effective learning. Practitioners are supported in this venture by a revised Ofsted inspection framework with a learning-centred approach.

The 2012 EYFS Statutory Framework is vague on defining both 'school readiness' and 'formal learning in year one'. However this allows leaders and practitioners to paint their own picture of what learning should look like in their school, and set engagement, motivation and thinking skills as their core business.

These core characteristics can be complementary, not contradictory, to Key Stage 1 provision. However practitioners need to think differently about the role of the teacher and learner, in order to avoid

> teachers adopting a technical approach, putting into practice a formulation based on particular activities or daily routines: an approach which inhibits professional development and the application of nuanced decision-making that is sensitive to the needs of individuals and the context in which they learn.
>
> (Stephen et al. 2009)

Good progress and good outcomes are most likely when teachers and school communities understand that lifelong learning aptitudes and attitudes are at the heart of planning, provision and practice.

> The one really competitive skill is the skill of being able to learn. It is the skill of being able not to give the right answer to questions about what you were taught in school, but to make the right response to situations that are outside the scope of what you were taught in school. We need to produce people who know how to act when they're faced with situations for which they were not specifically prepared.
>
> (Papert 1998)

References

Alexander, R. (ed.) (2009) *Children, their World, their Education. Final report and recommendations of the Cambridge Primary Review.* Abingdon: Routledge.

CACE (Central Advisory Council for Education (England)) (1967) *Children and their Primary Schools* (The Plowden Report). London: HMSO.

Callaghan, J. (1976) The Ruskin College speech. http://www.educationengland.org.uk/documents/speeches/1976ruskin.html (accessed 10 November 2012).

CBI (Confederation of British Industry) (2012) *Education Campaign: Ambition for All in Schools*. http://www.cbi.org.uk/campaigns/education-campaign-ambition-for-all/ (accessed 20 November 2012).

CCEA (The Northern Ireland Council for Curriculum Examinations and Assessment) (2007) Materials available online at: http://www.nicurriculum.org.uk/docs/key_stages_1_and_2/northern_ireland_curriculum_primary.pdf (accessed 25 November 2012).

Claxton, G. (2009) *What's the Point of School?* http://www.dystalk.com/talks/49-whats-the-point-of-school (accessed 9 January 2013).

DCSF (Department for Children, Schools and Families) (2009) *Independent Review of the Primary Curriculum* (Rose Report). Nottingham: DCSF Publications. Available at http://www.thrass.co.uk/downloadsdocs13.htm (accessed 25 November 2012).

DCSF (2005) Social and Emotional Aspects of Learning (SEAL). http://www.teachfind.com/national-strategies/social-and-emotional-aspects-learning-seal-improving-behaviour-improving-learning (acessed 1 January 2013).

DfE (Department for Education) (2012) *Statutory Framework for the Early Years Foundation Stage: Setting the Standards for Learning, Development and Care for Children from Birth to Five.* www.foundationyears.org.uk/early-years-foundation-stage-2012/ (accessed 1 January 2013).

Donaldson, M. (1978) *Children's Minds.* London: Fontana Press.

Dunn, R., and Dunn, K. (1978) *Teaching Students Through Their Individual Learning Styles: A Practical Approach.* Reston, VA: Reston Publishing Company.

Hymer, B. (2012) Passion, potential, performance. Paper presented at the North of England Education Conference, Leeds, January.

Isaacs, S. (1932) *The Nursery Years: The Mind of the Child from Birth to Six Years.* London: Routledge and Kegan Paul.

Kingsley, P. (2012) Michael Gove's National Curriculum reforms: where's the creativity? Education Guardian Series 'Doing things differently', *The Guardian*, 19 November.

Learning and Teaching Scotland (2009) *Curriculum for Excellence.* Available online at http://www.ltscotland.org.uk/curriculumforexcellence/curriculumoverview/index.asp (accessed 11 May 2010).

Nottingham, J. (2010) *Challenging Learning.* London: JN Publishing Ltd.

Ofsted (2012a) *The Framework for School Inspection from 2012.* http://www.ofsted.gov.uk/resources/framework-for-school-inspection-september-2012-0 (accessed 25 November 2012).

Ofsted (2012b) Good practice resource – an enquiry-based approach to learning: St Anne's CofE Primary School. http://www.ofsted.gov.uk/resources/good-practice-resource-enquiry-based-approach-learning-st-anne%E2%80%99s-cofe-primary-school (accessed 20 January 2012).

Ofsted (2012c) Good practice resource – preparing children to be 21st century citizens, contributing to sustainable communities: Southwood School. http://www.ofsted.gov.uk/resources/good-practice-resource-preparing-children-be-21st-century-citizens-contributing-sustainable-communit (accessed 20 January 2012).

Papert, S. (1998) Child power. Speech delivered at the eleventh Colin Cherry Memorial Lecture on Communication, Imperial College, London, 2 June.

Robinson, K. (1999) *All Our Futures: Creativity, Culture and Education.* The report of the National Advisory Committee on Creative and Cultural Education. London: DfEE/DCMS.

Siraj-Blatchford, I. and Sylva, K. (2004) Researching pedagogy in English preschools, *British Educational Research Journal,* 30(5): 713–30.

Stephen, C., Ellis, J. and Martlew, J. (2009). *Turned on to Learning 2: Active Learning in Primary One.* Applied Educational Research Scheme, Research Briefing 8. http://www.ioe.stir.ac.uk/staff/documents/AERSresearchbrief8.pdf (accessed 15 January 2013).

Suggate, S. (2007) Research into the Early Reading Instruction and Luke effects in the development of reading, *Journal for Waldorf/ R.Steiner Education,* 11(2): 17.

Sutton Trust (2011)*Toolkit of Strategies to Improve Learning: Summary for Schools, Spending the Pupil Premium.* http://www.suttontrust.com/research/toolkit-of-strategies-to-improve-learning/ (accessed 24 November 2012).

UNICEF (2008) *Getting Ready for School: A Child to Child Approach.* http://www.unicef.org/education/index_44888.html (accessed 9 January 2013).

Welsh Assembly Government (2008) *Play/Active Learning: Overview for 3 to 7-year olds.* http://new.wales.gov.uk/topics/educationandskills/earlyyearshome/foundation_phase/foundationphasepractitioners/playactive/?lang=en (accessed 16 November 2012).

Whitebread, D. and Bingham, S. (2012) *School Readiness: A Critical Review of Perspectives and Evidence.* TACTYC Occasional Paper 2.

Index

Locators shown in *italics* refer to diagrams, boxed examples, tasks and comments.